Stay the Course

Challenges to Salvationists
from the Book of Acts

Andy Miller III

For information, write:
The Salvation Army
USA Southern Territory
Literary Council
1424 Northeast Expressway
Atlanta, GA 30329

ISBN: 978-0-86544-050-0

Editors: Linda D. & Lynell Johnson, The WordWorking Shop

Cover Art: Erin Wyatt

Printed in the United States of America

Dedication:

To my wife, Abby, you know me,
strengthen me, and love me.
It's a joy to stay the course with you.

Contents

Part Three: Stay the Course

Ministry Resource: Two Dramatic Monologues

Introduction

You know how you test the temperature in a pool by barely dipping your toes in the water? Before I began intensively studying the book of Acts, I had only "dipped my toes" into it. When I needed to talk about conversion, I would go to Acts 9 for Paul's conversion. When I wanted to reflect on the role of the Holy Spirit and the growth of the Church, I would turn to Acts 2. If I needed to focus on unity and conflict resolution, Acts 15, about the Jerusalem Council, was the perfect passage.

When I plunged into studying Acts as a whole, it felt just like that—a plunge, a total immersion, like doing a cannonball into a pool. As I began to see the big picture and enjoy the details of some of the book's less well-known stories, I found a depth that renewed me for the fight. I came to admire Luke as a master storyteller and historian. At the beginning of his first volume, the Gospel of Luke, he describes how he *"carefully investigated everything from the beginning"* and *"decided to write an orderly account"* of the events surrounding Jesus' life. (Luke 1:3) Luke takes the same care to develop the events that follow Jesus' exaltation as the Church is born and matures in Acts.

My studies led to a sermon series, preached over three summers at the Lawrenceville, Georgia, Corps, also known as The Church on the Loaf (it's located on the Sugar<u>loaf</u> Parkway). I am deeply indebted to the dynamic, diverse, and Spirit–filled congregation there for their receptivity and contributions to the messages.

As a pastor in a Salvation Army corps, I naturally had Salvationists in mind as I wrote the sermons and converted them to chapters for this book. The focus and mission of the Army is centered on the work of God's Kingdom and the movement of the Gospel into every sphere of our world. That is the focus of Acts as well and the reason this book of the Bible is significant for us today. Because my audience will mainly be connected to the Army, I think there is an increased power in particularizing some of the ways that Acts challenges us as a movement and as corps. But the ideas in the book could easily inspire believers in other denominations as well.

Every sermon I preach emerges from dialogue with my partner in ministry and life, my wife, Abby. With regularity we talk through the text and its theological assumptions, the pastoral context of the corps we serve, and how our preaching connects the dots of these areas. Every sermon, and hence every chapter of this book, was developed in the context and joy of my shared ministry with Abby. Chapter 5 is based on two sermons in the series that she delivered.

This book takes a close (but by no means exhaustive) look at the major portions of Acts and challenges Salvationists to apply the principles found in those passages to their lives. The first part of the book, **Take Your Place,** focuses on the opening chapters of Acts, in which the people of God "take their place" after Jesus ascends and the Holy Spirit descends. The second section, **Unite ... Move ... Love,** describes how the early church became a "Church of Steel" that was "united" in mission, kept "moving" the Gospel forward, and "loved" others because of God's love for them. The final section, **Stay the Course,** relates the story of Saul, who became the Apostle Paul, and how he "stayed the course" to do his part in carrying the Gospel to the "ends of the earth." (Acts 1:8) In every section, I look not just at the text and what it means but also how the text can be applied to our lives.

You will also find two "bonus" dramatic monologues, first–person imaginative accounts from the points of view of two minor characters in Acts: Agabus and Titus. Feel free to use them in your own corps as resources for ministry.

It's my prayer that joining with me in the adventure that is the book of Acts will captivate you personally and inspire us all to "stay the course" for the sake of the Kingdom.

Acknowledgements

The worship committee at The Church on the Loaf (the Lawrenceville, Georgia, Corps) played a key role in helping develop titles and approaches to the messages that served as the basis of this book. Chris Corbitt, Joy and Cecil Sellers, and Nick and Roberta Simmons–Smith were early sounding boards for some ideas. Cecil Sellers developed a graphic for *Salvationists in Act(s)ion,* which the sermon series was originally called. Sue–Ann Jeffrey also was helpful in reading early edits.

Editors Linda and Lynell Johnson of The WordWorking Shop have been wonderfully helpful in advising me and reshaping the sermons into chapters. They have both helped me refine my "homiletical plot" in a literary context. My thanks as well to the USA Southern Territory's Literary Council, specifically Colonel Brad Bailey, Dan Childs, and Jeremy Rowland, for their support and encouragement of my writing.

I can't thank my wife, Abby, enough for her support of me and this project. Also, I must thank my three children, who make appearances in this book, because they demonstrate God's love to me in new and fresh ways each day.

Part One
Take Your Place

Chapter 1

Wait

Acts 1:1–8

Four thousand people attending the commissioning and ordination of Salvation Army officers sat in the large performance theater. My family's band was behind the curtain waiting to play.

We all were in our places, trying to breathe. Then I heard the curtain take a slight jolt. It raced up and we saw the crowd. Now it was time for action.

We experience or witness so many "points of action" like this one. The gun goes off to start the race. A 16–year–old starts the car ignition for the first time. College graduates throw their caps into the air. The curtain rises. It's time to "do something": to run, to drive, to start a career, to perform—to act.

The title of this part of the book is **Take Your Place**. In the early chapters of Acts, Jesus "takes His place" as He ascends to sit in authority at the right hand of God. The Holy Spirit "takes

3

His place" as He empowers God's people for mission. The disciples "take their place" in history and in God's movement. And today, we as Salvationists are called to **take our place** as a part of God's continuing story as it plays out through the universal Church.

Luke's story of the Church comes to us with a short, seemingly perfect title: "Acts." But other names have been suggested. An early manuscript calls the book "Acts of the Apostles," and that has a good ring to it. Yet it is Jesus who speaks throughout the book's first scene (vv. 1–11). Later, Jesus appears to Paul on the Damascus road. F.F. Bruce, one of the most prolific New Testament scholars of the last century, thought Acts should be titled "Acts of the Risen Jesus."

Still, with that heading, we would miss the book's emphasis on the Spirit empowering the early Christians, so perhaps it could be "Acts of the Spirit." But the role of the first person in the Trinity, God the Father, is also strong. Could it be called "The Acts of God"? Yes, that could work, but isn't it also the "Acts of the Church"? One of the challenges to that idea is that the word "Church" isn't how the disciples of Jesus refer to themselves. Instead they are called "followers of the Way." One scholar, Darrell Bock, suggests this title, "The Acts of the Sovereign God through the Lord Messiah Jesus by His Spirit on Behalf of the Way." I think I'll settle for Acts.

Acts is an epic that rivals any summer blockbuster movie. In Acts the early disciples take on the Roman Empire. They heal people and start a world–changing movement. They are beaten, shipwrecked, and bitten by snakes. In one scene, a king is even eaten by worms.

A Command from Jesus: Wait

But this exciting adventure begins in an unexpected way, as the disciples are challenged to **take their place**—by waiting. After Luke masterfully sums up what he wrote about in his "former book," the Gospel of Luke, he tells about the last scene of Jesus' ministry:

> On one occasion, while he was eating with them, he gave them this command: 'Do not leave Jerusalem, but _wait_ for the gift my Father promised, which you have heard me speak about. For John baptized with water, but in a few days you will be baptized with the Holy Spirit.' (1:4–5)

You can almost hear what the disciples are thinking: *All right, it's happening; we're going to get moving. John did great things, but now we understand what Jesus has been alluding to for these past 40 days. Let's go! Let's start our engines!* Then Jesus says, " ... but wait." Really? Wait?

As a Salvation Army, we are good at "action"; we are, in general, good at doing. An Army fights, it works—it "does." William Booth famously told his son, as they observed homeless people living below a bridge in London, "Do something, Bramwell ... do anything, set up a warehouse ... just go and do something." In keeping with Booth's urgency, our Salvation Army mission statement is pretty direct; we "preach the gospel and ... meet human needs in Jesus' name." As the Army, it is a challenge for us to wait.

The apostles obviously do not hear this word from Jesus about waiting. Perhaps sensing the climax of the contrast between John the Baptist and Jesus ("John baptized ... but in a few days you ... "), they were ready for action. For them, what

Jesus says is like a locker–room speech; they hear the promise, and they cheer. The next verse shows how they have missed the point.

> So when they had come together, they asked him, 'Lord, is this the time when you will restore the king-dom to Israel?' (1:6, NRSV)

They are ready to take on Rome. I can hear their minds work-ing at top speed: *Now we get it! You needed to die and be resur-rected and now you can do what we want, now you can restore Israel.* They are asking, "Is it time yet?"

A Part of Mission: Patience

Having small children gives me the privilege of hearing those words often. When our oldest was 4 years old, he approached me with his head slumped over. In a downcast voice, he said, "It's taking too long." Wanting to show sympathy, I responded, "What's taking too long?" Finally, after fussing for a minute or two, he confessed, "It's my birthday. My birthday is just taking too long." It was September and his birthday was not until May!

Like little Andy IV, the disciples are challenged to **take their place** and wait. Waiting is an "act" of submission. Patience comes with that action, and patience is a part of mission. This theme is not new to the Bible; many times we are called to be a "waiting" people. Famously Isaiah says, *"But those who wait for the Lord shall renew their strength, they shall mount up with wings like eagles, they shall run and not be weary, they shall walk and not faint."* (Isaiah 40:31, NRSV). We love the "run and not grow weary" part, and the "mount up with wings like eagles" part, but all of that is precipitated by waiting and trust-ing in the Lord. You don't run or fly unless you wait.

Will Willimon, a retired bishop of the United Methodist Church, says that our " ... waiting implies that the things which need doing in the world are beyond our ability to accomplish solely by our own effort, our programs and crusades. Some other empowerment is needed; therefore the church waits and prays."[1]

What do we mean by waiting? Could it be that we are maybe (1) not to jump in and tell God how He is supposed to work in the world? This is what the apostles were doing. Effectively, they were asking Jesus, "Won't you work with our plans and restore Israel right now?" Or it could be that by waiting, we will be reminded that (2) we are not God?

A Gift of Power: Worth the Wait

Waiting isn't all bad. Giving up on trying to control God's plans has its benefits. Jesus responded to the disciples' question:

> 'It is not for you to know the times or dates the Father has set by his own authority. But you will receive power when the Holy Spirit comes on you; and you will be my witnesses in Jerusalem, and in all Judea and Samaria, and to the ends of the earth.' (1:7)

If we wait for the Lord, we will receive power; a power that comes only from the Holy Spirit. While the disciples are wondering about the future, Jesus tells them about a mission for now. They will receive power, but not to restore Israel in the way they expected, as a mighty kingdom or established nation. They will be restoring it to what that nation was supposed to be in the first place—namely, a light to the nations. As you wait, the Holy Spirit will "come on you," and you will receive power to be my

---

1   William H. Willimon, *Acts* (Atlanta: John Knox Press, 1988).

witnesses, here and throughout the world.

St. John Chrysostom, a fifth–century church leader, is often regarded as one the greatest preachers of all time. He was known as the man with a "golden tongue" for his speaking. His homily on Acts 1 says this (he sounds like a Salvationist here):

> Just as soldiers are about to charge a multitude, no one thinks of letting them issue forth until they have armed themselves, or as horses are not allowed to start from the barriers until they have got their charioteer, likewise Christ did not allow the disciples to appear in the field before the descent of the Spirit, so they would be easily defeated and taken captive by the many.[2]

My personality and gifts are such that people have often said, "You could sell freezers in Alaska." I have thought, *Well, they could really use some up there.* But I don't want to do anything without the power of the Spirit. I don't want to be a good Army salesman; I don't want to be a good manager, leader, visionary—or anything—without the Spirit's guidance. I don't want my life to be explainable without the Holy Spirit. What about you? Have you **taken your place** and *waited* for the Holy Spirit to empower you?

---

2   Quoted in Thomas C. Oden and Francis Martin (eds.), *Acts: Ancient Christian Commentary* (Grand Rapids: Zondervan, 2006).

8

Chapter 2

Where You Sit

Acts 2:1–4

After the disciples have their last conversation with Jesus, they watch their Lord miraculously ascend into Heaven, where He will "take His place" at the right hand of the Father. The angels come on the scene to ask them an interesting question: *"Men of Galilee, why do you stand here looking into the sky?"* (1:11) The angels inform the disciples that Jesus will return again, in the same way they have just seen Him leave.

But the angels' question also implies: *Don't stand here any longer. It's time to move on, to receive that power Jesus promised you.* Jesus' ascension is the necessary precursor to all that will happen in the 28 chapters of Acts, as the disciples of Jesus begin to fulfill the mission statement they have been given: to spread the Word in Jerusalem, Judea, Samaria, and to the ends of the Earth.

But what did the disciples do first?

9

"They all joined together constantly in prayer ... " (Acts 1:14) While they wait, they pray. They don't wait and wonder; they wait in place and pray.

When Luke escorts us to the magnificent day of Pentecost, we find the disciples sitting and waiting. *"When the day of Pentecost came, they were all together in one place."* (2:1) In the previous chapter of this book, we learned that waiting is actually an action. Mohandas Ghandi once said, "Action expresses priorities." The disciples' action of waiting expresses their larger priority—obeying their Lord, Jesus.

Their sitting also brings a bit of tension to this scene. They may have been saying to themselves, *Why are we sitting here, God? There is a world to save, a plan to enact, and we haven't even moved out into Jerusalem, or even outside the walls of this house.*

Yet they continue to sit, waiting, as Jesus had commanded. Then, as Jesus had promised, the Spirit arrives in that room in a most dramatic way.

> *When the day of Pentecost came, they were all together in one place. Suddenly a sound like the blowing of a violent wind came from heaven and filled the whole house <u>where they were sitting</u>. They saw what seemed to be tongues of fire that separated and came to rest on each of them. All of them were filled with the Holy Spirit and began to speak in other tongues as the Spirit enabled them. (2:1–4)*

The Spirit doesn't come because of the disciples' abilities. The Spirit doesn't come as they reach a level of cultural acceptance. The Spirit doesn't come when they have the proper funding. The Spirit doesn't come when they have finished their strategic plan. The Spirit doesn't come because they have reached a high level of spiritual maturity. The Spirit doesn't come after they have completed their readings, their degrees, or their lunch. The Spirit doesn't come *when* they are perfect, *where* they might be someday or *where* they think they should be. The Spirit comes *where* they sit! Hallelujah!

It is interesting that in the telling of this great event, Luke never describes the disciples as "standing up," until they begin to excitedly tell others about Jesus. The first time Luke writes about someone standing up is when Peter stands to give the very first "sermon": *"Then Peter stood up with the Eleven, raised his voice and addressed the crowd."* (2:14) The Spirit came to the disciples where they were sitting. Then they stood, filled with that Spirit, ready to change the world.

The Spirit also comes to us where we are sitting. The Spirit comes if we wait in prayer, knowing that outside of our "house" is a world that needs to be changed. But like the disciples, we dare not go without the Spirit.

Today, God wants to fill us where we are, where we sit, where we kneel, so that we can be His voice.

Where do you sit? He wants to fill you, where you are. Maybe you are retired and wondering how God can fill and use you at this point in your life. Maybe you are about to start something new or you need to make a decision. Maybe you have been filled before and you know it, but you are "leaking."

Maybe you need to be filled again, D.L. Moody said, "A great many think because they have been filled once, they are going to be full for all time after, but O, my friends, we are leaky vessels, and have to be kept right under the fountain all the time in order to keep full."[1]

So ask the Lord to fill you—where you sit.

---

1   Quoted in Laurence W. Wood, *Truly Ourselves, Truly the Spirit's* (Grand Rapids: Francis Asbury Press, 1989).

Chapter 3

Proclaim

Acts 2:4-6

The Holy Spirit rushes in—with a mighty wind and tongues of fire—to enable the disciples to spread the Word about Jesus. The Spirit performs a miracle of speaking and hearing.

> *All of them were filled with the Holy Spirit and began to speak in other tongues as the Spirit enabled them. Now there were staying in Jerusalem God–fearing Jews from every nation under heaven. <u>When they heard</u> this sound, a crowd came together in bewilderment, because <u>each one heard</u> their own language being spoken. ... 'we hear them declaring the wonders of God in our own tongues!'* (2:4–6, 11)

The Spirit comes, where the disciples are sitting, so that they can speak of the "wonders of God" in a way that all those around them can hear—and there are many thousands who have thronged to the city for the Jewish "feast of weeks," Pentecost.

13

Connect to the Power Source ...

Admittedly I am not a tech guy; still, I have learned how to make basic functions of our house work. I am the one who handles all the cables and I am therefore responsible for the Internet service. Recently I was having trouble with our home wi–fi; I was confident that the problem was related to the router. After spending some time on the phone with the router company, they insisted I call our Internet service provider. Frustrated, and somewhat unwilling, I called. After waiting on hold, I finally spoke with someone. I explained that our Internet wasn't working. I felt the techie was asking some condescending questions. "Are you in the same room as the Internet source?" I responded with an air of confidence, "Of course." Next question: "Is the wireless router turned on?" I quickly and a bit shortly said, "Yes." The next questions frustrated me even more, "Is the AC adapter plugged into the wall?" "Yes." "Is the plug from the wall connected to the cable box?" Just I was about to confidently say yes again, I realized the answer to that question was ... embarrassingly ... no. I wasn't connected to the power source.

Problems in our spiritual life come when we are not empowered by God's Spirit. At that Pentecost celebration, the Spirit came to connect the disciples to the power source, which would enable them to speak in languages other than their own. *"All of them were filled with the Holy Spirit and began to speak in other tongues as the Spirit enabled them."* (2:4)

Enable is not a popular word in our culture. We don't want to enable people who have addictions to continue to abuse substances; we don't want to enable our children so that they won't "grow up." But the word *enable* simply means "make able." We don't make *ourselves* able. We can't fill ourselves or empower ourselves, but we are *made* able by the Spirit. The enabling of the Spirit happens where we sit; it comes to us as an act of grace.

When the Spirit is in us, we might be called "*in*–abled." This in–able–ness is not the kind we see played out in so many movies in which the major point seems to be, *I just need to trust myself, look inside myself and find the answers.* It's not some kind of "self–actualization." What the disciples learned in Acts 2 is that the answers for our world do not come *from* "in us," but they do come when the Holy Spirit *gets* in us.

… Then Witness

When the Holy Spirit came, the disciples were filled with the Spirit as they preached—and thousands were saved. The Spirit's work is about empowering people for mission: to witness to others. I love the word *mission* because it challenges us to see the big picture of God's work, but my only fear is that we don't lose *salvation* in our vocabulary. We are not "The Mission Army" or "The Missional Army." We are The *Salvation* Army, and God wants to fill us so we can lead people to Jesus. I truly believe that the Spirit led William Booth to change the name of our movement from "The Christian Mission" to "The Salvation Army" because this is what we are about. Booth said, "We are a salvation people—this is our specialty—getting saved and keeping saved, and then getting somebody else saved … "

We believe in the miraculous. We believe in moments of salvation. And we should make no apology about pursuing what Jesus has called us to do.

God gave the disciples a gift of speaking other languages for an evangelistic task: proclaiming the Gospel. That task belongs to us as well. **We have a message that needs to be heard**. In the midst of noise that threatens to drown out God's plan, we believe that God's message needs to be lovingly louder.

As you sit here today reading this book, I'm sure you can think of people in your life who have not responded to the

Gospel. (Think of those people right now.) Maybe they have taken a few steps in the right direction, but they are still at the edge of the pew waiting to put pressure on their feet and take a step toward the living God. Maybe they're not in church at all. They could be self–absorbed, clinging to materialism, filling a void for God through possessions, work, activities. Maybe they're self–described atheists or agnostics. Whoever "they" are, they need to hear the Good News.

Our "witness" might come in the form of relief, aid, justice, charity, or social ministry. In order to have our message—God's message—heard, maybe we give a meal to a hungry person. Maybe we show hospitality to a homeless family. Maybe we post an encouraging word on someone's Facebook page. Maybe we welcome a disabled child into our fellowship. Maybe we help to free someone from modern–day slavery.

Such ministries cost us money, time, parts of ourselves. But whatever the cost, we want people to hear. And for them to hear, we must **take our place** and proclaim.

Chapter 4

Poured Out

Acts 2:12–41

Moving is an emotionally and physically draining time for Salvation Army officers. In our case, our first appointment lasted five years. For that whole time, we "poured" ourselves into the ministry there. A short time after my wife, Abby, and I arrived at our second appointment, we were exhausted by the transition and drowning in all the work that needed to be done. We wondered, as we looked at all the challenges and opportunities of our new appointment, *Can we do it again? Do we have anything left to pour out?*

I imagine that the first Christians could have felt poured out by the time Peter got up to speak. They had been on a spiritual roller coaster. They had spent three sometimes exhilarating, sometimes trying years traveling with Jesus. They were devastated when this man they believed to be Messiah was killed on a Cross. They were overjoyed when He was raised and appeared to them. Then He left them—again. Then came the overwhelming experience of the Holy Spirit filling them, just as Jesus had promised. They suddenly found themselves enabled to speak in languages not their own to others who needed to hear about Jesus.

The Holy Spirit has given these "poured–out" disciples fresh energy. They are ready to change the world. However, they soon realize that the people around them don't understand the significance of what has just happened. *"Amazed and perplexed, they asked one another, 'What does this mean?' "* (Acts 2:12)

The crowd has not been completely won over by the sign of speaking in foreign tongues. Many are *"amazed and perplexed."* The Greek word used here for perplexed, *diaporeo*, could be translated "extremely confused." This same word is used (in the Greek translation of the Old Testament, the Septuagint, the text that Luke would have read and known) in the story of the tower of Babel in Genesis 11. After the world's languages had been confused, the people were *diaporeo*—greatly confused.

Too Much to Drink?

So were the people who heard the message of the disciples on the day of Pentecost. Then a group of "wise guys" in the corner chime in. *"Some, however, made fun of them and said, 'They have had too much wine.'"* (2:13)

I don't know what that moment was like for the 120 people God dramatically and miraculously used that day. I think it probably drained them even more. I can understand that. Even when I have sensed the Spirit using my preparation and preaching, I have found that it doesn't give me an emotional or physical pass. I am usually drained, spent, and worn down.

Imagine the disciples' response to the mocking of the crowd.

Probably one of the most amazing evangelistic miracles in world history has been performed through them—and people are laughing, saying, "I think they have had too much to drink." I can envision some disciples saying, "We've been through all this, God has used us ... I've poured myself out here, and still they don't get it. We're spent, we're tired, and if they don't get it yet, it's on them."

Peter, aware of this situation, aware too of his own denial and return to Jesus, hears the laughing and mocking and the question of the people, *What does this mean?* Then he rises to his feet, raises his voice and says:

> *'Fellow Jews and all of you who live in Jerusalem, let me explain this to you; listen carefully to what I say. These people are not drunk, as you suppose. It's only nine in the morning! No, this is what was spoken by the prophet Joel: "In the last days, God says, I will pour out my Spirit on all people. Your sons and daughters will prophesy, your young men will see visions, your old men will dream dreams." '* (2:14–17)

God says, through Peter, *"I will pour out ... "* I, the Creator, Preserver, and Governor of all things, I who crafted the seas and dry lands with my own hands (Psalm 95:5), *"I will pour out ... my Spirit on all people."* It's God's Spirit, not human energy, not effort, not intelligence, not willpower, that drives God's plan.

God Says: I Will Pour

As Peter quotes the prophet Joel, he does something interesting. He changes slightly what Joel said. Both the Hebrew Scripture (MSS–or Masoretic Text) and its Greek translation (Septuagint) have Joel saying, *"And afterward, I will pour out my Spirit ... "*

(Joel 2:28) But Peter says, "*In the last days, I will pour out my Spirit.*" Peter is saying, "*This* is the time!" God's Spirit is being poured out for a specific reason, namely, to call people into a relationship with Jesus. "Now is the day of Salvation," not next week.

These words, *poured out,* are rich and deep. One commentator says the "image is that of a torrential downpour that is poured out on a parched earth."[1] The world to which the Spirit came was a parched–dry world that desperately needed its thirst quenched. At the time Peter stood up, the world needed a "downpour of the Spirit."[2]

We were very careful to say in Chapter 1 that the book of Acts isn't just the acts of the Spirit, that Jesus is actively involved in this work too. The end of Peter's speech ties this up nicely as he brings back the language from Joel of "pouring out."

> '*God has raised this Jesus to life, and we are all witnesses of it. Exalted to the right hand of God, he has received from the Father the promised Holy Spirit and has poured out what you now see and hear. ... Therefore let all Israel be assured of this: God has made this Jesus, whom you crucified, both Lord and Messiah.*' (2:32–33, 36)

It is by the redemptive work of Jesus—that is, His life, death, descent, resurrection, ascension, and exaltation at the right hand of the God—that the Holy Spirit is poured out.

---

1   W.J. Larkin, *Acts IVP Commentary* (1995) quoted in Bock (see footnote 1 in Chapter 5).

2   The image of dried–up ground that is hard and not willing to be softened up could be used to describe people who are resisting the Spirit.

Need a Fresh Drink?

We too are thirsty, poured–out Christians who need the Holy Spirit to "pour into us." We **take our place** when we let the Holy Spirit do that. We are called to action, not alone, but through the Spirit.

A consistent message conveyed by the media these days is "Believe in yourself and you can do it." Here's the problem—if you believe in yourself, you will fail. You can't do it. You need answers for your problems that come from outside of you. Your own resources are already poured out. You will become exhausted if you try to carry the church's mission, the weight of your family, the expectations of others. You need God's Spirit to pour into you.

You may be thinking, *I just can't do it. I'm burned out. I can't give anymore.* You're right; you can't. But God's Spirit *in you* can.

Chapter 5

Catch the Kingdom Wave

Acts 4–5

Famed surfer Laird Hamilton, standing upright on his board, holds onto a rope as a speeding jet ski tows him along. Watching the video, you can almost sense the massive wave, but the camera is focused on him, so you can't tell how big it is. As Laird gains speed with the power of the jet ski, you see that he is poised on the crest of the wave. Then he lets go of the rope, and the jet ski moves out of view. As the camera pulls back, back, back, you see the surfer for what he is—a mere speck on a breaker so enormous it defies comprehension. The wave begins to curl, and Laird zooms down its face, propelled by the wall of water crashing around him, and exhilarated by the ride of a lifetime.

God's Kingdom is like a wave on the move. It is enormous, beyond our comprehension, and it's there whether we're ready to catch it or not. If we decide to ride this wave, we soon learn that it's traveling so fast that we can't do a thing in our own power. Our "paddling" simply won't do. We need the Holy Spirit to tow us along so we can get up to speed. Even when we catch the Kingdom wave, we still won't do the bulk of the work. We must simply be willing to ride the wave of what God is doing, exhilarated by its awesome nature.

The Rhythm of the Wave

How did the early apostles ride the Kingdom wave? As Acts 4 opens, we read that Peter and John were *"teaching the people, proclaiming in Jesus the resurrection of the dead."* The Sadducees were *"greatly disturbed"* by this, so they had the two men arrested and put in jail. But as they awaited their hearing, the Kingdom wave pressed on. *"Many who heard the message believed; so the number of men who believed grew to about five thousand."* (4:2–4)

Peter and John had caught everyone's attention in the first place by healing a lame beggar, in the name of Jesus and through the power of the Holy Spirit. (3:1–10) That was the "jet ski" that brought them to people's attention and allowed them to preach to large crowds about Jesus. The Sadducees couldn't deny the healing, but they demanded that Peter and John stop speaking or teaching in the name of Jesus. *"But Peter and John replied, 'Which is right in God's eyes: to listen to you, or to him? You be the judges! As for us, we cannot help speaking about what we have seen and heard.'"* (4:19–20)

The Kingdom wave was on the move, and nothing could be done to stop it. In fact, when Peter and John returned to their own people, and they heard what had happened, *"they raised their voices together in prayer to God."* (4:24) They asked the Lord to *"'enable your servants to speak your word with great boldness. Stretch out your hand and perform signs and wonders through the name of your holy servant Jesus.'"* After their prayer, the very meeting place was shaken, and everyone inside was *"filled with the Holy Spirit and spoke the word of God boldly."* (4:29–31)

The apostles and the early Church focused themselves on the Kingdom of God. Through these early chapters in Acts, we see them finding a rhythm of:

1. Gathering together, enjoying fellowship and the breaking of bread (2:42, 46)

2. Performing miracles (2:43; 3:7; 5:12)

3. Praying for boldness, signs and wonders (4:24–30)

4. Preaching and teaching (2:14, 42; 3:11–26; 4:33; 5:21, 42)

5. Sharing their possessions with each other (2:45; 4:32, 33–35)

We too can find our rhythm, a rhythm of fellowship and ministry, of prayer and proclamation, as we **take our place** in the action—riding the Kingdom wave because we realize that God's Kingdom is the hope for this world.

Seeing the Wave

In *Reaching for the Invisible God,* Philip Yancey writes about watching interviews with survivors from World War II:

> The soldiers recalled how they spent a particular day—one specific day. One sat in a foxhole all day; once or twice a German tank drove by, and he shot at it. Others played cards and frittered away the time. A few got involved in furious firefights. Mostly, the day passed like any other day for an infantryman on the front. Later, they learned they had just participated in

one of the largest, most decisive engagements of the war, the Battle of the Bulge. It did not feel decisive to any of them at the time, because none had the big picture of what was happening elsewhere.

As Christians, you and I are part of something huge. It's God's work in the world—His Kingdom being realized. That Kingdom turns things upside–down.

In Acts 5, we again find the apostles preaching boldly, adding many more to their number, healing the sick, and casting out demons. They have already been told several times (and we are only in the fifth chapter of Acts!) not to preach about Jesus. So again, they are arrested and put in jail. But when the Sanhedrin—*"the elders of Israel"*—send for the apostles, they are not there. The jail is locked, but they are not inside, because an angel of the Lord has set them free to *"tell the people all about this new life."* (5:20) The guards find the apostles *"standing in the temple courts teaching the people."* (5:25)

The apostles are brought before the Sanhedrin, and the high priest levels a charge against them: *"We gave you strict orders not to teach in this name. ... Yet you have filled Jerusalem with your teaching and are determined to make us guilty of this man's blood."* (5:27–28)

But the apostles remain defiant:

'We must obey God rather than human beings! The God of our ancestors raised Jesus from the dead—whom you killed by hanging him on a cross. God exalted him to his own right hand as Prince and Savior that he might bring Israel to repentance and forgive their sins. We are witnesses of these things, and so is the Holy Spirit, whom God has given to those who obey him.' (5:29–32)

Peter and the other apostles had turned the tables on the members of the Sanhedrin and put *them* on trial. The apostles had seen Jesus, risen from the dead, so they were not cowed by the people who killed Him. They knew that the plot to kill Jesus hadn't worked! The apostles had witnessed the coming of the Holy Spirit; they had healed people in the name of Jesus; they had seen thousands repent and follow Jesus as their Savior. They were filled with joy, and the Jewish council couldn't stop them. God had a claim on their lives that was much greater than the claim of this body of Jewish leaders. They had caught the vision of something big—God's Kingdom in motion—and they knew they were a part of it.

The Upside–Down View

At this point, the members of the Sanhedrin are furious and want to put the apostles to death. Not too surprising, is it? They really want to stomp out this Jesus commotion. But then one man stands up, a rabbi named Gamaliel. Much later in Acts (22:3), we learn that Gamaliel was Paul's teacher. He is a leading rabbinic figure—when he speaks, others listen. He reminds the elders of other "rebels" who have rallied men to them; but when they were killed, their followers scattered. He gives the Sanhedrin this advice about Jesus' apostles: *"Leave these men alone! Let them go! For if their purpose or activity is of human origin, it will fail. But if it is from God, you will not be able to stop these men; you will only find yourselves fighting against God."* (5:33–39)

Gamaliel's speech persuades the Sanhedrin, but before the apostles are released, they are flogged and ordered again not to speak in the name of Jesus. But when they go, they go *"rejoicing because they had been counted worthy of suffering disgrace for the Name. Day after day, in the temple courts and from house to house, they never stopped teaching and proclaiming the good news that Jesus is the Messiah."* (5:41–42)

They were beaten, yet they rejoiced. Why? *"Because they had been counted worthy of suffering disgrace ..."* This ancient society revolved around principles of honor and shame.[1] A great deal of value was placed on honor, which might be likened to our credit–rating system. A person who has good credit can buy more things and get better interest rates when they borrow—doors open for them. In the apostles' time, honor was something to be built up, like credit.

The leaders had beaten the apostles as a way of producing shame, in the hope that the shame might prove a deterrent and stop them from preaching. But in the apostles' upside–down Kingdom view, receiving punishment for their witness to Jesus was a great honor and cause for rejoicing. It's likely that the words of Jesus were ringing in their ears: *"Blessed are those who are persecuted because of righteousness, for theirs is the kingdom of heaven."* (Matthew 5:10)

The Crest of the Wave

When was the last time you suffered shame or embarrassment for the sake of the Gospel—for the sake of righteousness? Maybe it's been a while. Or maybe you never have. Robert Strawbridge, a Methodist circuit rider from the early 1800s, said, "If you're walking with the Devil, you will never run into him." Even if we aren't walking with the devil, we can be Christians who are just going through the motions. Then we wonder if God is working in our lives. We complain that He isn't speaking to us. We wonder

---

1   Darrel L. Bock, *Acts: Baker Exegetical Commentary on the New Testament* (Grand Rapids: Baker Academic, 2007).

why He isn't filling us with joy. We shouldn't sit still, wondering and complaining. We should seek Him, listen for His voice calling us to stand up for Him. The Apostle Paul wrote, *"I want to know Christ—yes, to know the power of his resurrection and participation in his sufferings ... "* (Philippians 3:10) That's how those first apostles became so bold; they knew Jesus because they had been with Him, both before he died and after He was resurrected. Because of that, they were willing to share in His suffering by suffering themselves for His name.

So how can we, who have never seen Jesus, **take our place** like the apostles? We can catch that Kingdom wave! Through the power of the Holy Spirit, we can have a relationship with Jesus so filled with joy that we will be unable to stop ourselves from witnessing in His name. We have to be prepared that when we speak about Him with boldness, as the apostles did, persecution may come. When it does, we shouldn't be *"ashamed of the Gospel,"* (Romans 1:16) but rather feel "honored to be dishonored."

When we ride the Kingdom wave, so many things can threaten to topple us. To keep our footing, we must keep our relationship with Jesus strong, through reading the Word, fellowshipping with one another, praying for boldness, and asking the Holy Spirit for guidance. Like the apostles, we must trust the Lord and be unafraid to suffer the consequences. We must trust that His grace is sufficient. In another upside–down Kingdom rule, His power is made perfect in weakness—and embarrassment and any other humiliation we might suffer. At those times, we may not be able to see the Kingdom wave—it's so much bigger than we are—but if we trust Him, we will be in for an exhilarating ride. **Take your place** at the crest of the wave, and get ready!

This chapter is a consolidation of two sermons given by Captain Abby Miller.

Part Two
Unite ... Move ... Love

Chapter 6

Church of Steel

Acts 6:8–15, 7:1–53

The people of any evangelical church—in our case, a corps—must be **united** in their goal of saving as many people as possible, must be willing to **move** in whatever direction that task takes them; most importantly, they must move, not for their own good or for the good of an institution, but because **love** compels them.

The church described in Acts is a model for us of a church **united** in mission. It is willing to **move** wherever, in whatever way God calls it. And it is motivated by the **love** of God, demonstrated in the life of Jesus Christ and driven through the power of the Holy Spirit. The church described in Acts is a "Church of Steel," a solid church that understands its purpose. It is a church that can take a hit and keep moving toward that goal.

Within that church are people of steel, people like Stephen. We meet him when the apostles choose seven Greek Jews, now

Christians, known to be *"full of the Spirit and wisdom"* (6:3) to assist them. In that list of seven, Stephen is singled out as *"a man full of faith and of the Holy Spirit."* (6:5) The apostles simply can't "do it all" any longer. They need to concentrate on the ministry of the Word, so they choose these men to take on the (equally important) responsibility of ensuring that none of the widows in the church, regardless of their ethnicity, are going hungry. But at least two of these men—Philip and Stephen— are doing more than waiting on tables and washing dishes.

We are told in Acts 6:8 that Stephen, *"a man full of God's grace and power, performed great wonders and signs among the people."* Just as Jesus had been opposed for doing such things, so is Stephen, as members of the synagogue begin to argue with him. But Stephen is so full of the *"wisdom the Spirit gave him as he spoke"* that his opponents cannot *"stand up"* against him. (6:10)

So his opponents resort to putting some others up to saying, *"We have heard Stephen speak blasphemous words against Moses and against God."* (6:11) False witnesses come forward to say, *"This fellow never stops speaking against this holy place* [the Temple] *and against the law. For we have heard him say that this Jesus of Nazareth will destroy this place and change the customs Moses handed down to us."* (6:13–14)

How does Stephen handle the accusations hurled at him? I believe that the responses given by this man of steel, which come in the longest speech in the whole book of Acts, will help us understand how to be a Church of Steel today.

First, Stephen is aware of his audience. He clearly hears the questions people ask and the accusations that are leveled against him and the church. He listens closely and responds wisely.

There is a story of a debate about Christianity that had been raging in a university classroom. One day when the students came to class, they found this statement written on the chalkboard in big letters: "Jesus is the answer." The next day, someone had written underneath it in smaller letters: "But what is the question?"

I believe that half the problem as to why we are not advancing, moving "forward to the fight," is that we are simply not listening to the questions of our culture—or even of our own friends.

N.T. Wright, a leading New Testament scholar from England, tells of his time as a chaplain at Oxford University. Every year the incoming freshmen from a certain college within the university were required to come to him to talk about "spiritual matters." Often the students were not Christians and would say things to him like, "This is a waste of my time because I don't believe in God." Wright would quickly answer, "Well, tell me about this God you do not believe in." Inevitably the students would describe a terrible God who was nothing like the true God. Wright would simply respond, "Well, I don't believe in that God either." He was willing to sit and listen so he knew where his students were in their thinking before he offered a response. Wright could then continue the conversation, giving students a picture of a different God, a God of holy love.

If we listen to people's questions before we begin our arguments about God, we might have just such an opportunity to talk about a God who loved us so much that He gave Himself in the person of Jesus Christ and is still present with us through the power of the Holy Spirit.

As a church, are we aware of our audience? Are we aware of our accusers? Or are we too concerned with providing excellent accommodations and benefits for ourselves? Are our pews, our seats, just for "us"? I think not. The empty seats in our buildings exist for sinners who are loved by God. And these people we exist to serve might have reasonable questions that we need to hear. Our strength doesn't come in what we do for ourselves. Our strength, our steel, comes from what we do for others—how we serve them, how we are willing to lay out all that we are for the good of our community, and perhaps most importantly, how we listen, even to our accusers.

Second, Stephen presents a vibrant history. The story Stephen tells is alive to him because he is steeped in the Scriptures. He knows that God's presence is not confined to a building such as the Temple or to Israel's narrow expectations.

Stephen has been accused of speaking against Moses. So he retells the history of Israel from Abraham to Joseph to Moses. To answer his opponents' accusation that he has spoken against the Temple, he outlines how it was raised and came through the line of David. Yet he adds that the Temple is not an adequate space to contain the glory of God. He cites Isaiah's recording of God's own words: " 'Heaven is my throne and the earth is my footstool. What kind of house will you build for me? says the Lord. Or where will my resting place be? Has not my hand made all these things?' " (7:49–50)

John Stott, a prominent thinker and evangelical pastor from England, wrote that the point of Isaiah's language is that the Temple/Tabernacle "should never have been regarded as in any literal sense God's home."[1]

Because Israel's history is alive in Stephen, he understands

---

1   John R. W. Stott, *The Message of Acts* (Downers Grover, IL: IVP Academic, 1994).

this point. Because Israel's history is alive in Stephen, he is able to call his accusers to account. He calls them *"stiff-necked people"* who, just like their ancestors, *"resist the Holy Spirit."* (7:51) When he goes even further, saying that they have *"betrayed and murdered"* the *"Righteous One"* and disobeyed the law, his hearers become furious. (7:52–54)

When his life was on the line and he was defending the Gospel, Stephen reached into his memory and recalled a vibrant history that enabled him to challenge his oppressors. If we stand alone and make our decisions autonomously, we won't be able to answer the critics in this lost world. If we, however, access the power of what Eugene Peterson calls a "biblical memory," we will draw upon three millennia of God's history and work in the world. Peterson explains that a Christian should "have David in his bones, Jeremiah in his bloodstream, Paul in his fingertips, and Christ in his heart" and consequently will not be dependent on the "momentary feelings and the experience[s] of the past week."[2] Stephen's connection to this kind of history via his biblical memory enabled him to impact his audience of accusers. Maybe this presentation of a vibrant history caught the attention of the young scholar, Saul of Tarsus, holding the murderers' coats.

Third, Stephen is in touch with the exalted Christ. As the anger of the mob grows, he looks up to Heaven and sees *"the glory of God, and Jesus standing at the right hand of God."* (7:55) He sees Jesus, God who was incarnate, who lived and taught among the people, who suffered, was tried and humiliated, died, and was resurrected to eternal life. This is the same Jesus who

---

2   Eugene Peterson, *A Long Obedience in the Same Direction* (Downers Grove, IL: Intervarsity Press, 2000).

ascended to the Father and intercedes on our behalf. The same Jesus, when Stephen looks to Heaven, appears to him as He stands at the right hand of God.

Stephen's last day on Earth was much like the last days of His Lord. Both Jesus and Stephen were "tried," suffered the testimony of false witnesses, and spoke of the Temple made with hands that would be destroyed. Both were accused of blasphemy and killed for answers to their accusers' questions. And both, as they died, asked God to forgive their murderers.

Both Jesus and Stephen, as they were dying, committed their spirits to God. But their words were slightly different. As Jesus died on the Cross, He said, *"Father, into your hands I commit my spirit."* (Luke 23:46) Stephen said, as he was being stoned to death, *"Lord Jesus, receive my spirit."* (Acts 7:59) Luke is making a very clear point about Jesus and His Lordship. Jesus is back where he belongs, standing at the right hand of the Father, waiting to receive Stephen's spirit.

Stephen is in touch with the exalted Christ. So is the church in Acts. To them, Jesus is not simply a revolutionary figure, a sacrificial symbol, a solid teacher, a good man. He isn't simply resurrected, and He is more than ascended: He is recognized as Lord! He is exalted! He is leading the Church through the power of the Spirit. That Church is a Church of Steel, forged in the Spirit.

Our corps should be churches of steel too, in touch with the exalted Christ. We stay in touch with Jesus when we proclaim the Good News of the Gospel and perform works done for the good of the world in Jesus' name.

Jesus said that when we feed the hungry, clothe the naked, minister to the sick, and visit prisoners, we are ministering to Him. (Matthew 25:34–40) To be the church, we must be doing these things. I believe church happens when we meet someone who is homeless and provide her with a place to stay. I believe church happens as we provide a food basket and a prayer to a needy family. I believe church happens through League of Mercy, as we visit and stay in contact with the sick. I believe church happens as our Community Care ministries visit people in prison. I also believe church happens as families teach their children about Jesus, as children in Adventure Corps shout "Adventure in Christ!" and as Sunbeams and Girl Guards learn and share their sacred promises. And I believe the church is active and moving most specifically when we witness, telling other people about the good things that Jesus has done for us and is doing in our lives today.

Stephen was a holy example of what a member of the Church of Steel looks like. Thousands, if not millions, of martyrs have followed his lead. The power of the Gospel touches our lives in such a dramatic fashion that we can't help but desire to **unite** behind Jesus' and Stephen's example. Despite the challenges that come from a fallen world, we have to **move** as His Church into places where God's light is absent. We unite and move, not for our own motives, but because **love** compels us, just as love compelled Stephen.

Chapter 7

Keep Moving

Acts 8

Sometimes, at the end of a long day, you may feel as if you can barely summon enough energy to put one foot in front of the other. It's as if your feet are asking, "Do we have to keep moving?"

The very idea of moving can be draining. It means change, a disruption from what we are used to doing. It means we will no longer be where we were.

Philip was a man who was always on the move. We first meet him in Acts 6 when he is one of those chosen to serve the Greek widows, who are not being fed.

Stephen, another of the men chosen that day, became the first Christian martyr. As a result of Stephen's stoning (Acts 7), the church in Jerusalem, made up at this point of Jews who believed in Jesus, was *"scattered throughout Judea and Samaria."* (8:1) We are told that *"those who had been scattered* preached the word wherever they went." (8:4) Among those spreading the word, Philip "went down to a city in Samaria and proclaimed the Messiah there." (8:5)

In Luke's unfolding of the early movement of the Church, Philip moves from behind the scenes to the main stage. He draws crowds as he proclaims the Messiah, and he performs many signs. Through the Holy Spirit, Philip causes "impure spirits" to come out of people, and he heals so many who were paralyzed and lame that there is "great joy in that city." (8:6–8) He even sways the followers of Simon, a man who had boasted of his own greatness and practiced sorcery to produce his own signs. Simon's followers "believed Philip as he proclaimed the good news of the kingdom of God and the name of Jesus Christ" and "they were baptized, both men and women." (8:9–12) Then Simon himself leaves his life of sorcery behind and is baptized because of new faith in Christ. "And he followed Philip everywhere, astonished by the great signs and miracles he saw." (8:13) Because he has **kept moving in the Spirit**, Philip converts one of the people least likely to embrace Jesus.

Marching Orders

In the midst of this tremendous ministry, Philip gets marching orders. "Now an angel of the Lord said to Philip, 'Go south to the road—the desert road—that goes down from Jerusalem to Gaza.' " (8:26)

Philip has no idea why he is being sent to that road, but because the Lord has called him to go, he immediately starts out. He doesn't hesitate. He has to leave Samaria, where, despite the hostility of the Samaritan people toward anything Jewish, he has been wildly successful in proclaiming God's Word.

Philip is commanded to move from an experience of

fruitfulness to a "desert road." Yet he obeys God's order to move.

Abby and I faced a huge change in our lives when we felt God leading us to officership and to fulfill that calling in the USA Southern Territory. When the moment came for us to receive our first appointment and we learned that it would be in Texas, I admit I felt a little like Philip being told to go to that desert road.

The appointment system in The Salvation Army keeps officers moving. I overheard one soldier say, "Officers come and officers go; praise God from whom all blessings flow!" Not only do officers move, but the world also keeps moving; culture keeps moving; the Church keeps moving; our families keep changing. Our sense of belonging and home can be disrupted as we adjust to where we are.

Philip Yancey, in his book *Grace Notes,* tells of a conversation he was privileged to have with a long–time seminary president, Vernon Grounds. The 90–plus–year–old man spoke about the ups and downs he had experienced in his Christian walk. Then he said, "I have an unquestioning confidence in God's ability to accomplish whatever God wants ... when you have been around as long as I have, you have to. Like the Chinese philosopher riding backwards on a donkey, we only understand life looking back." Grounds had been moving with the Spirit all his life, even when he couldn't see results until long afterward, if at all.

So Philip is on the desert road, where he encounters *"an important official in charge of all the treasury of the Kandake (which means 'queen of the Ethiopians')."* (8:27) The man is riding in a chariot, and the Holy Spirit interrupts Philip's journey to say, *" 'Go to that chariot and stay near it.' "* (8:29) Philip doesn't just move toward the chariot; he *runs* up to it. When he overhears this foreigner reading from the book of Isaiah, Philip knows he is reading a prophecy about Jesus, and he offers to explain it to him.

Because Philip **kept moving with the Spirit**, he had the opportunity to witness about his Lord and to baptize the man. Then, when Philip's work was done, the Spirit suddenly took him away, moving him first to Azotus and then to many other towns as a traveling evangelist—a man always on the move.

'On the Road' Encounters

Acts is the second half of a two–volume work by Luke. The first volume is the Gospel of Luke and the second describes the work of God through the power of the Holy Spirit in the lives of the disciples as the Church expands. In his Gospel, Luke tells an "on–the–move" story that takes place after the resurrection. Two disciples are walking on the road to Emmaus and Jesus appears with them. As the three walk along together, He unfolds what the Scriptures say about the Messiah.

In Acts 8 we also have a traveler who needs an interpretation of the Scriptures. I think it is telling that these stories take place while people are on the road, while they are moving. When we **keep moving with the Spirit**, God can and *will* unfold all that He wants us to know about His plans for the world.

Philip was told to move for a variety of purposes. When the Church was scattered across Judea and Samaria, Philip **kept moving with the Spirit** and went to a city in Samaria. When he met a sorcerer named Simon, Philip **kept moving with the Spirit** and drew Simon's followers and then Simon himself to the Lord. When the angel of the Lord told him to go to a desert road, Philip **kept moving with the Spirit** even though he didn't know why he had been called there. When he was on that road and saw the Ethiopian official in the chariot, Philip **kept**

moving with the Spirit and witnessed to the man. When the man asked for more information about what God was saying in Isaiah 53, Philip **kept moving with the Spirit** and unfolded the meaning of Scripture while he rode along with him in the chariot. When Philip arrived in a new town, he **kept moving with the Spirit** to boldly preach the Word. We too must keep moving—but only if we know that we are moving with the Spirit.

Moving with Kingdom Focus

A strange scene unfolded when my wife took our son Andy IV to the doctor for his regular checkup. Abby described a moment when Andy's eyes welled up and he could hardly contain himself. When the doctor was finished, Andy had a question for him, "How many shots will I get today?" Our family doctor is probably used to this question and the angst of young people, so he quickly and cheerfully responded, "None!" As soon as this reality hit, Andy started crying. The doctor didn't understand until my wife explained that she and Andy had developed a little ritual where he gets a smoothie after getting a shot. Both of my boys actually look forward to shots because they are aware of the smoothies coming their way! They are willing to do anything to get their reward.

Philip too was motivated to do whatever it would take for his desired outcome: seeing others come to faith in Jesus Christ. His outcome was Kingdom–focused.

It never ceases to amaze me how my boys (ages 8 and 6) can be jumping off of walls imitating Spiderman, but the moment we ask them to help us clean, they act as if they are paralyzed. Spiderman becomes a sloth. Words that I would normally long to hear come from their mouths: "I'm tired." It's not that they are really tired. It's just that they are being asked to change their plans from playing to cleaning, and they don't like it. They don't want to obey their parents' call to move.

God wants you to **keep moving** in your spiritual life, even if you don't feel like it.

- When you feel as if you are in a dry, desert place in your life—**keep moving with the Spirit**.

- If you are at a new stage in your life— **keep moving with the Spirit**.

- When you feel that the next step might be painful—**keep moving with the Spirit**.

- If you sense that your faith is not strong—**keep moving with the Spirit** anyway.

Maybe you don't hear the Spirit calling you to move. If not, it's time to ask the Spirit to make Himself clear to you. Maybe you—and the people of your corps—need to spend more time in prayer, Scripture reading, and fasting so that His will becomes clear. Then, be ready, as Philip was, to go into hostile territory; to go when and where the Spirit calls you, even if it's to a "desert" road; to witness to the "whosoever" and welcome those new people into the Kingdom.

That's the way we'll help ourselves, our corps, and our Army to **keep moving with the Spirit**.

Chapter 8

Breathe

Acts 9:1–19a

There is no G–rated version of this story. A mob rushes a Greek Jew named Stephen, who has just testified about Jesus and accused them of murdering Him. They drag him outside the city. They throw their coats at the feet of a Pharisee named Saul and pick up rocks to stone Stephen. Saul doesn't pick up a rock himself. Yet he doesn't do anything to stop the mob. In fact, Scripture says, *"And Saul approved of their killing him."* (8:1)

No one knows how Saul arrived on the sidelines that day, but he was there, moving against God's plan.

If you asked this Saul what he loved more than anything, he would have said the Law. He hated the followers of Jesus because they proclaimed Him the long–awaited Messiah. To Saul, that meant they were a threat to that Law, and he would lead the charge to stamp out this renegade branch of Judaism.

Just as the mob *"dragged"* Stephen away (7:58), Saul himself, on a one–man campaign to *"destroy the church,"* *"dragged"* away Jesus' followers, both men and women, and put them in prison. (8:3)

Saul was so **united** with this purpose that he dedicated his life to destroying the young movement. He didn't realize that both the Law he loved and the followers of Jesus he sought to move off the map were part of a Church of Steel, the Church that the Spirit of God was strengthening despite Saul's attempts to eliminate it.

For the early Church, "It was the best of times, it was the worst of times ... " (Charles Dickens). The Way, as the Church was called at that time, was expanding. The Holy Spirit was powerfully working: people were being saved, healed, and freed from prison. The apostles were confronting the establishment. The new Church was moving mightily. But as soon as Stephen was killed, that Church was scattered. (8:1) It became "the worst of times" for this early movement of God. And Saul was actively involved in making it so.

The book of Acts reads like a great story, with heroes and villains. Saul, at this point in the story, is one of those villains.

Meanwhile, Saul was ... breathing out murderous threats against the Lord's disciples. He went to the high priest and asked him for letters to the synagogues in Damascus, so that if he found any there who belonged to the Way, whether men or women, he might take them as prisoners to Jerusalem. (9:1–2)

'Breathing Out' Against God

There is some haunting language here. This persecutor, Saul, was *"breathing out murderous threats"* against the Christians. It's an image of someone completely controlled by hate and frustration. Saul is breathing out against what he sees as an attack on God's covenant with His people—the Law; he is breathing out against this man called Jesus. What he doesn't realize is that he is breathing out against God.

Breathing is the most basic of human functions. So when Saul "breathes out" hatred, it becomes the essence of his personhood.

It is not uncommon for people in our world to be like Saul, breathing out threats against God's movement. Breathing out against God is deep and personal. It can mean actively scorning or even persecuting people who believe in Jesus. Or it can mean leading a lifestyle that moves against God's plan.

You might believe in God. You might even tell people you will pray for them in hard times. You might sporadically come to church. You might occasionally do Christian–ish things. But could you be a functional atheist, what Oklahoma City Pastor Craig Groeschel calls a "Christian atheist"? That's someone who claims to believe in God but lives as if He doesn't exist, someone who effectively says, "I've got it. I don't need God."

Our society too, with its "all–about–me" attitude, can move against God's plan. You might believe you don't have to be concerned about how your decisions impact others, just as long as your personal needs are met. You might think you don't have to be concerned about the environment, the marginalized person, or the people who walk into The Salvation Army at the lowest point in their lives. Our world is spinning in this direction; it breathes out against God and His plan just as Saul did when he dragged off followers of the Way.

A Breath of Hesitation

In the midst of this persecution, a disciple of Jesus named Ananias hears from the Lord. And instead of breathing out, he takes a deep breath in. Likely someone who had experienced the outpouring of the Spirit in Jerusalem, he has a vision in which he hears the Lord call his name: "Ananias!" *What a pleas-ant surprise!* he must be thinking. He responds immediately, *"Yes, Lord."* (9:10) We can imagine that he's excited about what the Lord will say next. *Maybe God is going to call me to take the Gospel to a tropical island!* But soon his, *"Yes, Lord,"* becomes a questioning, *"Lord [?]"* (9:13) We can sense disappointment and fear from Ananias when he hears the Lord's instruction: *"The Lord told him, 'Go to the house of Judas on Straight Street and ask for a man from Tarsus named Saul … ' "* (9:11)

We can imagine Ananias' shoulders lifting with his next breath in, which must have been calculated and painful. His response shows his extreme reluctance. *" 'Lord,' Ananias answered, 'I have heard many reports about this man and all the harm he has done to your holy people in Jerusalem. And he has come here with authority from the chief priests to arrest all who call on your name.' "* (9:13–14)

The apprehension must have been plain on Ananias's coun-tenance. He is a living example showing us that **uniting** and **moving** with God's plan can be challenging. God's call to **love** means we have to love even those who have sought to destroy us. But it also means that through us, God's love can call a sin-ner "breathing out" against God to repentance.

Maybe you are not breathing out against God. But you could be questioning him, just as Ananias did. He wondered if God could really be trusted to use Saul. "God, are you sure about this?" You could be saying, "Are you sure you want me in this ministry, God?" "Uh … you know that I don't like to do this kind of thing." "God, don't you realize that I would rather be somewhere else?" You may wish for another vocation, another life, another way of ministry. Like Ananias, you may have heard clearly what God has called you to do. Yet, with a fearful heart, you breathe in and wonder if you have the courage and strength to do it.

Deep Breaths of the Spirit

Ananias has a decision to make in this moment: Does he unite and move with the Spirit or go his own way? Does he show love to someone who was, until a short time ago, ready to kill him? The answer for a member of the Church of Steel has to be **unite, move,** and **love.** So Ananias takes a deep breath of the Spirit and follows the Lord's command.

God says to Ananias: *"Go! This man is my chosen instrument to proclaim my name to the Gentiles and their kings and to the people of Israel. I will show him how much he must suffer for my name."* (9:15–16)

We can imagine Ananias taking another deep breath before he obeys God and sets off to meet Saul.

Ananias is in good company.

- Abram no doubt took a deep breath when God told him to pick up everything and go to a new land.

- Noah must have taken a deep breath when God told him to build an ark in the middle of the desert.

- Moses likely took a deep breath when God told him to raise his arms for the Red Sea to part.

- Joshua probably took several deep breaths before he ordered the priests and his army to march around Jericho for seven days. And on that last day, he may have even held his breath as the trumpet blasted and the shout rang out.

- Mary had to have taken a deep breath before she agreed with the Lord to have a baby by the Holy Spirit.

- Simon Peter probably took a deep breath before he dared to say who he thought Jesus was.

But each of those people **moved** in response to God.

- Abram went to the new land, and God's plan to save the world began with his obedience.

- Noah built the ark, and the floodwaters came.

- Moses lifted his staff and the waters parted.

- Joshua's army marched seven times around Jericho and the walls came "a–tumblin' " down.

- Mary obeyed and gave birth to the Son of God.

- Simon Peter boldly declared Jesus as Messiah, and the Lord said to him, " ... *I tell you that you are Peter, and on this rock I will build my church ...* " (Matthew 16:18)

In Acts 9:17, despite having taken that deep breath of hesitation, Ananias exhaled and **moved** in obedience toward Straight Street.

> *Then Ananias went* [he **moved**] *to the house and entered it. Placing his hands on Saul, he said, 'Brother Saul, the Lord—Jesus, who appeared to you on the road as you were coming here—has sent me so that you may see again and be filled with the Holy Spirit.'*

Ananias expresses his faith out loud. He doesn't say "Saul, you scoundrel, you persecutor, what are you up to?" Instead, he addresses this person who had breathed out threats against God as *"Brother Saul"* because he knows that Saul has had a dramatic meeting with the Lord Jesus.

> *As [Saul] neared Damascus on his journey, suddenly a light from heaven flashed around him. He fell to the ground and heard a voice say to him, 'Saul, Saul, why do you persecute me?' 'Who are you, Lord?' Saul asked. 'I am Jesus, whom you are persecuting,' he replied. 'Now get up and go into the city, and you will be told what you must do.' (9:3–5)*

Who Are You, Lord?

Saul had been breathing out threats against a concept, against a fringe group of uneducated Galileans. But here, on the road to Damascus, a Person confronts him. He sees the resurrected Jesus, and he is blinded by His light. Then Jesus calls out his name! *"Saul, Saul, why do you persecute me?"* Saul asks, *"Who are you, Lord?"* (9:4–5)

We all must ask that question at some point in our lives. You have to have the guts to face the question for yourself: Who is Jesus for you? Is He truly Lord? Have you **united** all your desires, all the hopes and dreams of your life—behind this Jesus who loves you? If not, you have to ask, "What do I do with Jesus?"

When you are witnessing to people who don't know Jesus, you can hang around with them for hours and discuss the problem of evil in the world. You can listen to people's questions and argue with them. Such conversations have their place. But at some point, you have to help unbelievers ask this question of themselves: "What do I do with Jesus?"

Saul had already decided that he would follow Jesus. But when Ananias laid hands on him, Saul breathed in the Holy Spirit and *"Immediately, something like scales fell from Saul's eyes, and he could see again. He got up and was baptized, and after taking some food, he regained his strength."* (9:18–19)

It's hard to believe that the Saul who had been so full of hate would come to **love** Jesus more than the Law, would **unite** with his former enemies, and, filled with the Holy Spirit, would seek to **move** throughout the Mediterranean world spreading the Gospel he had once despised. Yet it happened. He became the Apostle Paul.

Whether you are living wholeheartedly for God or living a life that breathes out against God, He wants to breathe into you. He wants you to move to join his plan to save the world. He wants you to love sinners as much as He does. He wants you to unite with others who are on the same journey. Are you like Saul or like Ananias? Are you living a life against God or simply questioning him? It's time to **unite** with God's people, **move** with the Holy Spirit, and **love** Jesus just as Ananias and Saul chose to do.

Chapter 9

Unite in Courage and Love!

Acts 9:19b–31

The "Church of Steel" sounds like it must be a church made up of strong, confident, ultra-gifted believers. But look at Saul and Ananias. Saul was a persecutor of Jesus who was humbled, blinded, and weakened by hunger after his encounter with the living Lord. Ananias was a follower of Jesus, a disciple, who questioned the mission the Lord gave him because he was afraid. Saul was told to wait in a house on Straight Street, and he did what he was told. Ananias was told to go to that same house and lay hands on a man who, if they had met just a few days before, might have dragged him off to prison or even killed him—but Ananias did what he was told. Both men were weak, but both ultimately obeyed the Lord. And because they did, "Brother Saul" received his sight and, more importantly, the Holy Spirit.

After the scales fell from Saul's eyes and he was baptized, *"At once he began to preach in the synagogues that Jesus is the Son of God."* Saul needed great courage to do this because everyone knew who he had been: *"Isn't he the man who raised havoc in Jerusalem among those who call on this name?"* The people didn't trust Saul at all. They asked, *"And hasn't he come here to take [the Jewish Christians] as prisoners to the chief priests?"* Yet, instead of being fearful, Saul *"grew more and more powerful"* as he proclaimed Jesus as Lord. In a matter of days, Saul became a man of great courage and confidence. (9:20–22)

Courage in Community

Recently my wife, Abby, read *The Wizard of Oz* with our children. Listening in, and reading a chapter or two myself, I was reminded how tough it is to resist that lovable character, the Cowardly Lion. In the movie version, there's a drum roll. Then, coming to a moment of clarity, the Lion exclaims:

> What makes a King out of a slave? Courage!
>
> What makes the flag on the mast to wave? Courage!
>
> What makes the elephant charge his tusk in the misty mist or the dusky dusk?
>
> What makes the muskrat guard his musk? Courage!
>
> What makes the Sphinx the seventh wonder? Courage!
>
> What makes the dawn come up like thunder? Courage!
>
> What makes the Hottentot so hot?
>
> What puts the "ape" in apricot?
>
> What have they got that I ain't got?
>
> Courage!

It is through his journey with a girl from Kansas, the Tin Man, and the Scarecrow that the Cowardly Lion discovers that he can be "king of the for-EHHHST" [vibrato and all].

In one way, this story is off–target, and in another, it perfectly hits the mark. The Lion is basically told that he indeed has courage; he just doesn't know it. He is told to simply look inside himself. That solution is wrong for the Lion and wrong for us. We can't simply look inside to find ourselves.

Saul begins to find himself through something that comes from outside of him. That something is a Someone. The person of Jesus comes to him. It is his experience with Jesus that brings Saul to a place of **moving** forward. For us, too, courage to move comes as we experience the power of the Lord in our lives.

We, as part of the Church of Steel, recognize that we are weak. We are sometimes unsure about our future. But Jesus has a plan. We sometimes lose focus. But Jesus helps us to see. We are sometimes fearful. But Jesus gives us courage.

What the story of Dorothy and her friends does get right is that courage is more likely to be birthed and to flourish in community. It was through their relationship as a group of flawed individuals struggling to find the Wizard that they discovered the resolution to their challenges.

We often hear about Saul on the road *to* Damascus, but for most of my life I have neglected to think about Saul *in* Damascus. We learn that *"Saul spent several days with the disciples in Damascus."* (9:19) It's likely that Ananias, his first brother in the Lord, was one of the people nurturing him in the earliest days of his Christian life. Right after those days, he began to preach in the synagogues about Jesus. As a preacher, Saul wasn't going it alone. He had the power of the Spirit and a community that **united** behind him to spur him on, to give him the courage to preach boldly.

Here's a quick biographical summary of what happens next: Saul spends time preaching in Damascus, goes to Arabia, then after three years comes back to Damascus before going to Jerusalem. (Galatians 1:17–18) We don't hear that whole story in Acts. Luke leaves out the three-year period and concentrates on Saul's second sojourn in Damascus. This time, Saul falls under persecution and his life is in danger. He escapes with help from a **united** community: believers lower him in a basket through a hole in the city wall. The church in Damascus stands with him, even when it's dangerous to do so.

We Can't Go It Alone

Saul sets out for Jerusalem. When he arrives, he immediately wants to link up with those who were apostles before he was— the men who had been Jesus' companions on Earth. But he meets strong resistance. *"When he came to Jerusalem, he tried to join the disciples, but they were all afraid of him, not believing that he really was a disciple."* (9:26)

What would make Saul want to persist in trying to join the Church under these circumstances? After all, Saul had had a powerful experience with Jesus; the Spirit was using him; he had been effective in spreading the Gospel. So why did he need the church at Jerusalem?

You might—no, you will—hear from some people who have found the Lord: "Jesus is enough for me, I don't need the Church. They are all a bunch of hypocrites anyway." Saul could have felt this way. But, from his experience in Damascus, he knew the importance of being part of something bigger than himself—and not just any something. It had to be the Church, the community of believers.

The Church of Steel cannot be experienced in solitude. Our

Christian experience must be verified by connecting to the universal Church. This connection does not diminish our experience but validates it.

Some of the best stories in our world are those that relate to the theme of communities uniting for a task. *The Wizard of Oz* is about a group of unlikely friends who unite for each other; *Star Wars* is about a group of people uniting to take on the Empire; *Lord of the Rings* is about a fellowship of people moving to save their world; and my favorite movie, *Hoosiers,* is about a group of farm boys, a loose–cannon coach, and an alcoholic assistant coach coming together to win the Indiana state basketball championship. These examples are all pale reflections of what our Triune God has done in creating the Church as His partner in redeeming the world. The Father sent the Son, who in turn sent the Spirit to bring about this transformation through His Church, a team uniting for a purpose.

Inclusive Love

On a slow Wednesday night in the middle of the summer, a handful of us witnessed a beautiful moment in a corps Bible study. After the lesson was done, "Shawn" asked for prayer because he was moving back to his hometown. Shawn had come in a few months earlier because he was sleeping in his car and had heard that we could help him. He happened to come on a Wednesday night. He was welcomed right in to Bible study, then made his way to Men's Club.

We helped Shawn find a safer place to stay than his car. He came to church the next Sunday and went to the altar. A retired officer who didn't know his story prayed with him, and he accepted Jesus as his Savior (later we learned that he had grown up entrenched as a Jehovah's Witness). Two faithful soldiers took him to lunch that first Sunday. Small business owners in the corps hired him for a few days so he could get some money in his pocket. Then he got a new job.

On this somewhat slow Wednesday several months later—when, to be honest, I hadn't felt like making my way to the corps building—Shawn looked around our group and said, "I'm going home, so will you all pray for me?" We did. Then he hugged us, thanked us, and headed out the door. Recently we learned that Shawn got involved in the Salvation Army corps in his home-town and has become an active soldier there. The point is that a community had surrounded Shawn, who became a follower of Jesus. His life was transformed. When we become a part of the Church of Steel, we come together as a body and show the love of Christ to others.

The church would have missed the opportunity to welcome Saul had it not been for a person who lived to encourage and lived in courage—Barnabas. After the disciples rejected Saul for fear of their lives, it was Barnabas who stepped out in faith. *"But Barnabas took him and brought him to the apostles. He told them how Saul on his journey had seen the Lord and that the Lord had spoken to him, and how in Damascus he had preached fearlessly in the name of Jesus."* (9:27)

This church in Acts that unites and moves also **loves**. Barnabas, through love, had a vision of what could be. Like Barnabas, we need to see the potential in people—often people whom others reject or fear. Because of Barnabas, Saul could **move** *"about freely in Jerusalem, speaking boldly in the name of the Lord."* (9:28)

Courage to be the Church of Steel comes when we are **united** with other believers, as Saul experienced with Ananias, with the church at Damascus, with Barnabas, and, eventually, with the church at Jerusalem. We need to unite for the cause of the Church: proclaiming the good news of Jesus.

As Paul (once Saul) went about preaching and teaching, he almost always traveled with a companion. The only place he went alone was Athens. While he gave a great speech at Mars Hill (Acts 17), this was probably his least successful "appointment." Paul wrote letters to all of the churches he visited or established. He wrote to the churches at Thessalonica, Corinth, Ephesus, Philippi, and Colossae, and the region of Galatia, but there is no letter to Athens, the place he went alone.

'I Am Spartacus!'

The Church of Steel needs to be united for another reason: we are in a war against the forces of darkness. *Spartacus* is a classic movie that retells the historical account of the great Roman slave rebellion in 71 B.C. Spartacus was a highly trained gladiator who escaped and led other slaves to freedom. As news of his rebellion grew, thousands of slaves joined his cause and followed him through victories and defeats.

Near the end of the movie, a massive Roman army under the command of Senator Crassus (Laurence Olivier) captures the rebels. Although Crassus does not know what Spartacus (Kirk Douglas) looks like, he suspects that he is one of the prisoners under guard. In full Roman uniform, Crassus gallops up to the mouth of the valley where the prisoners are being held and shouts an offer to them: they can escape death by crucifixion if they turn Spartacus over to him.

Spartacus studies the ground for a moment, then nobly begins to rise to his feet, intending to turn himself in. But before he can do so, his comrade to the left stands and calls out, "I am Spartacus!" Then his comrade to the right stands and calls out,

"I am Spartacus!" As the real Spartacus looks on, comrade after comrade in his slave army rise to their feet and call out, "I am Spartacus!" until there is a chorus of thousands united.

Those slaves showed what it means to be the Church—standing as one and identifying with our Lord even though it could mean our own end.

When you read this story, can you see it as a metaphor for your corps? Are we courageous warriors for the Lord standing together, **united,** against the foe? Do people know us as followers of Jesus because of the **love** they see in us for one another? It is only when we have such love and unity that we will be able to courageously **move** "forward to the fight" for souls.

Chapter 10

Don't Hesitate

Acts 10–11

At the beginning of Acts, Luke records the risen Jesus telling His followers that they would be witnesses *"in Jerusalem, and in all Judea and Samaria, and to the ends of the earth."* (1:8) The early stories in Acts show the first disciples spreading the Gospel first in Jerusalem, then throughout Judea and Samaria as they are scattered by persecution. We read about heroes of the faith like Stephen, a man of steel who united with the exalted Christ as he was martyred for his faith; Philip, who kept moving with the Spirit wherever God sent him; and Saul, one of the Church's chief persecutors, who literally saw the light of Jesus and, surrounded by a community of believers who supported him, began to spread the Gospel himself.

Now we come to Acts 10, a turning point in Luke's narrative, conceptually and theologically. The story told here, of Peter and a Roman military figure called Cornelius, is the beginning of the proclamation of the Gospel to the Gentiles, and to *"the ends of the earth."*

Just before this story begins, Peter has been about his business, spreading the Gospel among the Jews. People turned to the Lord as, in the name of Jesus, Peter healed people and even raised a woman named Tabitha (Dorcas) from the dead. That happened in Joppa, where Peter stayed at the home of a man named Simon. (Acts 9:32–43)

Peter and the other apostles thought they knew exactly what their work was: reaching their own people with the message of Jesus. But God had another, much bigger plan. So at this point Luke's story changes direction. He leaves Peter where he is, in Joppa, and moves north to Caesarea, to introduce us to Cornelius, a Roman centurion (an officer leading 100 men) of the Italian regiment. (10:1)

We're told that Cornelius and his family were "God–fearing." That means that they believed in the one true God and tried to live moral lives; in fact, we learn that Cornelius *"gave generously to those in need and prayed to God regularly."* But Cornelius never expected what happened one ordinary day at three in the afternoon: in a vision, he sees an angel of God who addresses him by name! Cornelius is terrified; he responds, *"What is it, Lord?"* The angel tells him that his prayers and gifts have brought him to God's attention and instructs him to send men to Joppa to bring Peter back to Caesarea. Cornelius obeys immediately. (10:2–8)

While the men are on their 30–mile journey to Joppa, Peter receives his own, very different vision. He sees " ... *heaven opened and something like a large sheet being let down to earth by its four corners."* The sheet is filled with all kinds of four–footed animals, as well as reptiles and birds. A voice says, *"Get up, Peter. Kill and eat."* Peter doesn't obey immediately; he hesitates and objects: *"Surely not, Lord! ... I have never eaten anything impure or unclean."* Some of the animals are clearly ones that Peter, as an observant Jew, is forbidden to eat; doing so would be repulsive to him. But then the voice speaks again: *"Do not call anything impure that God has made clean."* That vision and those words, unforgettable to Peter and to us, are repeated three times before the sheet is taken back to heaven. (10:10–16)

While Peter is thinking about the meaning of the vision, he receives a direct word from the Holy Spirit letting him know that three men are waiting for him at the door of the house. The Spirit says, *"So get up and go downstairs. Do not hesitate to go with them, for I have sent them."* (10:17–20)

When I have read this story, I have always tended to concentrate on Peter's initial hesitation. After all, he did say, *"Surely not, Lord!"* On the other hand, when he received the command from the Spirit to go where three strangers would lead him, he obeyed without question. Peter invited the men into the house as his guests for the night and the next day he went with them. **Peter didn't hesitate to *unite* himself with God's plan.**

To be **united** means to be connected for a purpose. We can unite with coworkers, with a sports team, with those who agree with us on an issue, with a personality—even with a popular preacher.

As believers who are part of the Church of Steel, we unite for a purpose. We who are Salvationists don't unite to be part of a club of people who wear uniforms on Sunday morning. We unite with one another, like all members of the universal Church of Steel, because we have a common purpose: inviting people to follow Jesus, to learn of His plan to redeem the world and of His desire to redeem every person. We unite with God's plan. This focus is what drives Peter past his hesitation. It's what **unites** him with God and **moves** him to leave his familiar surroundings. When he unites with God's plan, the Spirit causes his heart to beat with **love** for the world.

In a recent study of choirs in the journal *Frontiers of Neuroscience,* Swedish researchers report that as choir members sing together, their heart rates become connected to their breathing patterns and to the tempo of the music. The singers become physiologically united; their hearts actually start beating together.[1] As believers, our hearts need to beat together with the heart of God.

I recently had occasion to drive down the street where my paternal grandparents once lived. As their former house sped by my window, I remembered a critical moment in my life that happened there. I had flown into town to visit my grandparents and then to drive to south Georgia to visit a girl whom I hoped would marry me (turns out she did!). My grandparents let me borrow their car for a few days to make the trip. As I started the ignition, my grandfather took my hand and put an additional set of keys in it. He said very casually, "You will need these." He was giving me that car!

I can still see my grandfather's arms resting on the top of the window as he said, "Andrew, the air conditioning just stopped working, but you can roll down the windows." I thought, "Well, you know, your first car can't be perfect." Then, just as I was about to put the car into drive, he yelled, "Andrew, the gas gauge doesn't work either, so every 250 miles you will need to stop." I began to realize that my grandparents had given me a true lemon. Still, when I had awakened that morning, I had not owned a car. Now I did. Do you think I said, "Grandpa, if this car is that bad, I don't want it"? Not a chance. I had my own car, and I was moving. He could have told me anything, and it wouldn't

---

1   http://www.npr.org/blogs/health/2013/07/09/200390454/when-choirs-sing-many-hearts-beat-as-one

have mattered to me because I had my own wheels! On my way back to St. Louis, the car broke down twice. A few weeks later the paint started to wear off, and I had to duct tape the bumper on. Still, I was moving with a purpose; I was on my way to see Abby because I didn't hesitate to accept this "lemon" of a gift.

Peter had been given a vision and an order, and he had to move with a purpose, and without hesitation, to unite with God's plan. He had no idea what the future would look like when he went with those men to meet Cornelius, a Gentile. As a Jew, Peter wasn't even supposed to associate with a Gentile, let alone visit one in his home or, especially, share a meal with him. But when he did those things, he was given an opportunity to preach the Gospel. When he did, he introduced the Church—and the world—to the boundless salvation possible in Jesus. He united the Church with its future.

Cornelius, who had himself followed the orders of the Lord in sending for Peter, gathers a crowd of Gentile relatives and friends at his home to meet with their guest. (10:24) He tells Peter that they are all there "in the presence of God to listen to everything the Lord has commanded you to tell us." (10:33) What an opening for a preacher! **Peter doesn't hesitate to _move_ in sharing the full Gospel story.**

When Peter begins to speak, it's clear that he has been contemplating the implications of the vision the Spirit sent him—and it's not just about what he can and cannot eat. _"I now realize how true it is that God does not show favoritism but accepts from every nation the one who fears him and does what is right."_ (10:34–35) Then Peter gets right to the point, building on what the people gathered there have already heard: _"You know the message God sent to the people of Israel, announcing the good news of peace through Jesus Christ, who is Lord of all."_ (10:36) Peter doesn't refer to Jesus as merely "that guy from Nazareth."

Just as he had once said, *"You are the Christ"* to his Master, Peter now uses that term to emphasize that Jesus is the Jewish people's long–awaited Messiah. But he also says that Jesus is "Lord of all," which means that He initiated this important work on Earth to redeem the world. That description also has great significance for Peter's hearers because even though they are not Jews, he is letting them know that Jesus can be their Lord too.

Peter goes on to declare that he was a witness to the miracles Jesus performed. He presents the Gospel in clear terms: he tells how Jesus was killed, raised from the dead by God, appointed by God as *"judge of the living and the dead,"* and that *"everyone who believes in him receives forgiveness of sins through his name."* (10:39–43)

Right then, even as Peter was speaking those words, *"the Holy Sprit came on all who heard the message."* (10:44) Peter might have been thinking, *How dare the Holy Spirit interrupt? Doesn't He know that I have another three points and a poem?*

But the Spirit must have been with Peter, too, for he said nothing more; he just allowed the Spirit to do His work. Those who had come with Peter, a group of *"circumcised believers,"* were dumbfounded to see that the *"gift of the Holy Spirit had been poured out even on Gentiles."* (10:45)

It's a beautiful moment. Just like at Pentecost, the new believers are filled with the Spirit and speak in tongues, praising God. (10:46) Word about what has happened spreads quickly. But instead of receiving the news with joy, Peter's friends, who believe that only circumcised Jews can be saved, are quick to criticize. They don't see what the Spirit has done, only what Peter has done. When he gets back to Jerusalem, the "circumcision group" jump on him immediately, *"You went into the house of uncircumcised men and ate with them."* (11:1–3)

Peter's friends are acting the way parents sometimes do: "You went where? With those people? You know better than that!"

The easiest thing for Peter to do would be to back down. But he doesn't even think twice. **Peter doesn't hesitate to *love* by standing up for the truth.** He tells his friends the whole story about the vision God sent him and the vision God sent Cornelius; about going to Cornelius's home; about sharing the Gospel with Cornelius and his family and the immediate result: the outpouring of the Holy Spirit. He says, *" … the Holy Spirit came on them as he had come on us at the beginning."* (11:4–15)

Recalling what the Lord said about the importance of being baptized with the Holy Spirit, Peter then says what he thought when he saw the Spirit being poured out on those people in Caesarea: *"So if God gave them the same gift he gave us who believed in the Lord Jesus Christ, who was I to think that I could stand in God's way?"* (11:16–17)

That was it for the circumcision group. They couldn't argue with that. Not only didn't they raise any further objections, but *"they praised God, saying, 'So then, even to Gentiles God has granted repentance that leads to life.' "* (11:18) Peter's courageous witness before his friends changed their minds, through the power of the Spirit.

Are you hesitant to **unite** with God's plan, to turn yourself completely over to Jesus? Are you hesitant to **move,** even though you know what God is telling you to do? Are you hesitant to **love** by standing up for the "whosoever" who have come to Jesus?

Think about Peter. He didn't hesitate to **unite** himself with God's plan, to **move** when God told him to move, or to **love** by standing up for the newest Gentile believers. As a result, the Gospel began to be spread "to the ends of the earth." Don't we want to keep that glorious legacy going?

Don't hesitate!

Chapter 11

Come Along

Acts 11:19–30

We've just witnessed that beautiful moment when the Apostle Peter returns to Jerusalem telling what the Holy Spirit has done in the household of Cornelius, a Roman centurion living in Caesarea. At first, Peter's friends in the circumcision group are ready to hang him out to dry for committing the sacrilege of breaking bread in the house of a Gentile. But when Peter describes the scene—much like a mini–Pentecost—his friends break out in praise, acknowledging that Gentiles too can be saved. They are **united** in purpose.

We've looked at this pivotal story as the launching pad for the Church of Steel to begin its mission to bring the Gospel to the "ends of the earth." That adventure was happening in other places as well. Luke tells us that *"those who had been scattered by the persecution that broke out when Stephen was killed traveled as far as Phoenicia, Cyprus and Antioch ... "* Then Luke adds a key phrase, *"spreading the word only among Jews."* (11:19)

Tension Point #1: The Word Spreads to the Gentiles

Next comes a big *"however,"* which signals a sharp contrast. We learn that some of the evangelists, *"men from Cyprus and Cyrene"* who went to Antioch, *"began to speak to Greeks also, telling them the good news about the Lord Jesus."* (11:20)

To our modern ears, hearing that some evangelists are preaching outside the Jewish community sounds perfectly logical and natural. We recognize that *"all have sinned and fall short of the glory of God."* (Romans 3:23) And in Antioch, there are 480,000 other sinners besides the Jews! Why not try to reach them? In Salvationist terms, we would put it that we want to reach the "whosoever."

But such an idea was new for the fledgling Church. Even though the Church "elders" in Jerusalem had agreed (in principle) that Gentiles, too, could be believers, that didn't put an end to the controversy.

Tension Point #2: Jerusalem Investigates Antioch

As the disciples were moving with the Spirit in Antioch, loving the Gentiles they encountered, *"The Lord's hand was with them, and a great number of people believed and turned to the Lord."* (11:21). The next verse says simply *"News of this reached the church in Jerusalem, and they sent Barnabas to Antioch."* (11:22) A more accurate, literal translation of that verse is *"News of this was heard in the ears of the church in Jerusalem."* Could it be that not everyone in the home church welcomed the news? We learn later in Acts that the circumcision party is still alive and well, so could it be that they did not approve of this mission to the Gentiles? Maybe they felt that Peter's experience with Cornelius and his household was an exception to the rule. Perhaps they felt that the Greeks hearing the Gospel in Antioch would need to be circumcised before they could become true followers of Jesus. None of that is spelled out in the text, but it appears that the leaders of the Church felt they had to send Barnabas to check out just what was going on in Antioch.

Let's try to imagine what the evangelists at Antioch thought when the news reached their ears that Barnabas was on the way. They might have wondered why the Jerusalem church needed to be involved. After all, they knew that the Lord's hand had been with them, and great numbers of people had come to know Jesus as Lord. The evangelists might have worried that the elders in Jerusalem were calling their mission into question and thinking that they weren't doing things the proper way. They surely knew about the circumcision party and could have feared that Barnabas was coming to convey the message that the new believers had to be circumcised. Or, they might simply have wondered, *Why does Barnabas have to come here at all?*

Well, if the evangelists did worry about Barnabas, their fears were unfounded. And if the Jerusalem Church had sent Barnabas to Antioch to expose any improper teaching, they sent the wrong man. We learn that *"When he arrived and saw what the grace of God had done, he was glad and encouraged them all to remain true to the Lord with all their hearts."* Barnabas was *"a good man, full of the Holy Spirit and faith, and a great number of people"* came to know Jesus as Lord through his ministry. (11:23–24) He **came along** and encouraged and strengthened what was already happening. With the help of Barnabas, the church at Antioch was **coming along** too.

Tension Point #3: Saul Joins the Team at Antioch

Then we learn that *"Barnabas went to Tarsus to look for Saul [later known as Paul], and when he found him, he brought him to Antioch."* (11:25–26)

The church at Antioch had done quite well even before Barnabas arrived. With him, the church continued to grow explosively. No doubt, the original evangelists and the new believers at Antioch soon became very comfortable with this new teacher, Barnabas. But when they learned that he was about to leave and bring back yet another evangelist, Saul, they might have said to themselves, *We're doing really well with our team. Why do we need this guy Saul?* But if that's what they were thinking, they soon changed their minds. We learn that *"for a whole year Barnabas and Saul met with the church and taught great numbers of people."* Saul **came along**, and the church continued to be strengthened.

It's interesting to speculate about what the people in Jerusalem and Antioch thought, about how they might have wrestled with issues as the Church experienced growing pains. Some of that speculation comes from our understanding of human nature, and of churches in particular.

Like the elders in Jerusalem, I occasionally hear about The Salvation Army's work in other communities and wonder if it is valid. I learned recently about a corps that has meetings that have no planned program or order of service. Like Quakers, the soldiers (and officers) sit in the chapel and wait for the Spirit to reveal what is supposed to happen. There is a part of me that says, *They need an order of worship; they need to sing certain songs; the preacher must prepare ... after all, I prepare for my sermons—how dare they simply wait upon the work of the Spirit?* But what I also learned about this church is that it is reaching out to the community and people are being brought to a healing relationship with Jesus as a result of their ministry. If the mission of The Salvation Army, the mission of the Church of Steel, is to "preach the Gospel," this church is fulfilling the mission.

In The Salvation Army, we've all experienced the transition from one set of officers to the next. Many of us think, as people in the Antioch church might have thought, *We're doing really well. Why do we need someone else to come along?* Yet we soon learn that our new officers care just as much for the church as we do. And the mission continues.

The first believers in Antioch said to the small, local Jewish community, "Come along." Some likely did that. Then they expanded their message to include the hundreds of thousands of Gentiles living in the city as well. They said, "Come along." Large numbers did that. Then Barnabas arrived from Jerusalem, and when the believers saw that he was all about encouraging and strengthening the work, they said, "Come along, Barnabas, and teach us." Many thousands more came to know Jesus and His Lordship. Then the believers said to yet another teacher, Saul, the man Barnabas brought to them, "Come along and lead us to new heights of understanding the richness of the Gospel and how it is to be proclaimed *'to the ends of the earth.'*" And the church continued to grow.

The people of the church at Antioch didn't just move according to their own expectations. They welcomed and worked through new challenges; they were willing to **come along** with the Spirit's work in their community. They didn't hold onto the comfort level they had when they first met Jesus. They were aware that hundreds of thousands of people in Antioch needed to hear the Good News of the Gospel. And they went to their city and said, "Come along!" They moved through any tension they might have felt because they were willing to move with the Holy Spirit.

I believe that this is the essence of the community that calls itself The Salvation Army, a church that is part of the apostolic line, part of the Church of Steel. Our primary motion, our primary activity, our primary reason for existence is to say to anyone we meet, "Come along."

We need to be like the church at Antioch. The believers there were willing to move with the Spirit, even when it produced something uncomfortable, like unbridled growth. (That's a challenge every growing church faces.) They moved with the Spirit, even when a new leader they didn't know came along. They moved with the Spirit because they were eager to reach the world with the Good News of their Savior, Jesus Christ.

The people of the church at Antioch experienced a great adventure that gave them the vitality to move with the Spirit in their city, not for themselves, not for their own comfort, but because they were **united** in their passionate desire to share the Gospel.

I think that we, The Salvation Army, need to be willing to **come along** with God on a great adventure with the Spirit and His movement in the world. After all, we have a Savior who **came along** for us in His incarnation, life, death, resurrection, and ascension.

The church in Antioch persisted despite great change because it was connected to this same Jesus and to the Spirit. Notice that when we read about what was happening in Antioch, it doesn't say that the people of the church were telling others the good news about their programs, their music, their beautiful new building, or their covered-dish dinners. It says they were *"telling them the good news about Jesus."* As they did, the Spirit **came along,** doing a powerful work among the people as they heard and accepted the Good News.

When we **come along** with God's plan for our world, we're ready to allow the Spirit to work in and through our lives—just as He worked so long ago in the city of Antioch.

Chapter 12

What Are You Called?

Acts 11:26c

Sometimes a name change can alter the way we view reality. In 1977, fish merchant Lee Lantz traveled to Chile and "discovered" the toothfish, a species the locals considered too oily to eat. Thirty years and a name change later, Chilean sea bass is so popular with American palates that it's almost on the verge of extinction.

Another fish, known as the dolphin fish, is unrelated to the mammal of the same name. But diners still balked at ordering it. So in the mid–1980s, restaurants started using its Hawaiian name: mahi–mahi. All thoughts of Flipper were forgotten.

When the California Prune Board realized the words prune and "laxative" were inseparably linked in people's minds, they changed "prunes" to "dried plums" in 2000. Sales went up. In a documented focus group, tasters preferred dried plums to prunes.

To sell oil extracted from the rapeseed plant, marketers had to deal with the unfortunate name. In 1988, the FDA approved a name change to canola oil, and sales skyrocketed.

Back a couple of thousand years ago, Jesus' disciples were known as followers of the Way, which many considered what we would call a cult. Then, one day, someone came up with a nickname for those followers, a name which eventually came to define Jesus' followers worldwide.

In the sweeping story of the church at Antioch, where everyone **came along** with the Holy Spirit, and "great numbers" accepted Jesus as Savior, that nickname is found in one short sentence that seems tacked on, almost as an afterthought. The sentence, not even half a verse, is found at the end of Acts 11. I'm calling it 11:26c.

As Luke was building his two–volume work of Luke–Acts, I imagine he probably had a variety of drafts. Scribblings of source material written on smaller parchments may have surrounded his desk as he worked on his Holy Spirit–inspired masterpiece. Maybe he had drafted a whole page on the details of this part–verse, but we don't see that. Instead, he simply says, in the famous 11:26c, *"The disciples were called Christians first at Antioch."* These disciples who **united** and **moved** and **loved** their community were the first people in human history to be called Christians.

What Was Meant as an Insult ...

This was not likely a term of endearment. It was probably an expression coined to mock the disciples in Antioch. I can imagine them selling *War Crys* as they proclaimed the Good News about Jesus in bars, where the stench of humanity was strong and the activity was anything but holy. Maybe there was a protester who said, "Get out of here you ... you ... you ... what *are* you guys called anyway?" Maybe one confident believer said, "We are disciples of Jesus Christ, who is the Savior of the world. He gives us hope as we anticipate the resurrection of our bodies. We believe that this Jesus is the Lord of all creation, that He was with God in the beginning, that He is the eternal Word of the Father, that He is the Son of God, the Messiah—the Christ—and we are his disciples." Then the tough protester, impatient with such a long–winded explanation, might have shot back, "I said what are you *called?*" Maybe Barnabas summarized, "We are followers of the resurrected Jesus, who is the Christ." So the person looking to mock them might have said with a sneer, "Fine, *Christians,* get on out of here."

Sometimes people struggle to find the right way to insult somebody. When I was a child, a young adult from our corps was giving me a hard time. I got so mad at him that I couldn't find the right words to say, so, thinking I was insulting him, I stammered, "You're, you're, you're … *beautiful.*" As a 5–year–old boy who resisted anything pink, pretty, and Barbie, I thought this was a pretty good insult.

Some followers of Jesus in those early days might have reacted badly to the "insult" of being called Christians. We can imagine the shoulders of one of those disciples slumping momentarily or one of the evangelists nearly weeping at such mockery of the Lord. But we can also imagine one of the believers saying, "Wait a minute. They're right. That's exactly who we are—Christians. We are a people whose whole identity is found in this man named Jesus, who was not simply a man, but God's Son and Messiah—the Christ. The power of His Spirit is working among us right now. So yes, we are indeed Christians."

No Superhero Christians

My fear is that we may look at these disciples of Jesus as "superhero" Christians. Just as we know that Superman's ability to fly is beyond our human ability, so the actions of Peter, Saul, and Barnabas may seem beyond what God could possibly do through us. But we must not fall into this trap.

In a commercial advertising athletic apparel, Michael Jordan, who is generally regarded as the greatest basketball player in history, challenges a group of young players:

> Maybe it's my fault. Maybe I led you to believe it was easy when it wasn't. Maybe I let you think my highlights started at the free throw line and not in the gym. Maybe I made you think that every shot I took was a game winner, that my game was built on flash and not fire. ... Maybe I led you to believe that basketball was a God–given gift and not something I worked for every single day of my life. Maybe I destroyed the game [for you] ... or maybe *you're* just making excuses.

He is expressing his awareness that some young people could point to his "superhuman" achievements as a reason to not give their maximum effort.

Sometimes we may think that there is a status in Christianity we simply can't achieve. We may think that only certain people can really be spiritual or holy. A friend of mine was asked to lead the prayer initiative for his church's capital campaign. He was a planned giving director for a charity and felt that he was being approached because of his technical skill. He responded to the pastor by saying, "I am not really a prayer guy." To his shock, the pastor slammed his shoulders against the wall and yelled at him, "Who told you that? And why do you believe it?"

This dramatic move snapped my friend out of his lethargic spiritual life; today, he is a spiritual giant.

We are prone to think that some people are simply "born" with spiritual sensitivity, just as Michael Jordan was "born" to play basketball. That's simply not true. People become fully involved, fully engaged followers of Jesus, not because they are "naturally" more spiritual than anyone else but because they die to themselves and surrender their lives to Jesus and His movement in the world.

These followers of Jesus, these so–called Christians at Antioch, didn't say, "Hey, we got a name," and start calling themselves by it. The title "Christian" is used only three times in the New Testament. In Acts 26:28, King Agrippa responded to Paul's defense of the activity of Jesus in the world, saying, *"Do you think that in such a short time you can persuade me to be a Christian?"* Then, in 1 Peter 4:16, the apostle writes, *"If you suffer as a Christian, do not be ashamed, but praise God that you bear that name."*

Are We 'Altogether Christians'?

Today, the title *Christian* often provokes a negative response. To many people, it means that we hold a particular set of social and political views, sometimes expressed in hateful ways. As a result, some of us have felt—and I have been in this camp at times—that we shouldn't even use the title "Christian." But maybe what we need to do is show the world what it really means to be a Christian. If we're going to do that, we have to know it—and live it—ourselves.

John Wesley preached a famous sermon called "The Almost Christian." The huge popularity of this sermon at the time is hard to describe. The only thing I can compare it to is how quickly a Justin Bieber tweet spreads among middle–school–age girls. Pamphlets of this sermon were published and distributed throughout England. Wesley's radical idea was that some people were "Almost Christians" while others were "Altogether Christians."

> The supreme question, therefore, still remains: Has God's love been poured into your heart? ... Do you love your neighbor as yourself and as Christ loved you? Do you love even your enemies? ... Do you have redemption through his blood, even the remission of your sins?... Awake, therefore, you that sleep, and call upon your God. Call upon him now, while he may be found. ... May we move beyond being merely Almost Christians. We can become Altogether Christians.[1]

The church at Antioch was certainly a fighting force of Altogether Christians. Is that true of us? What would your spouse or your closest friends say about your Christian walk? Does your schedule indicate that you are making Jesus a priority? Does your checkbook demonstrate that you are a follower of Christ?

The name *Christian* is vital—if it calls us to recognize that we are not our own, that *"we were bought at a price"* (1 Corinthians 6:20), that we belong totally to Jesus. Elyse Fitzpatrick explains that "Christians are, by definition, people who have someone else's identity. They're called Christians because they've taken the identity of someone else: the Christ."[2] It's not like we have been robbed of our identity; instead, we receive the amazing

---

1   Kenneth Cain Kinghorn, *John Wesley on Christian Beliefs* (Nashville: Abingdon Press, 2002).

2   Elyse Fitzpatrick, *Because He Loves Me: How Christ Transforms Our Daily Life* (Wheaton, IL: Crossway, 2008).

added benefit of a life in Christ. Fitzpatrick calls this an "identity gift." Identifying with Christ and his plan for the world **unites** us with other Christians and the *"great cloud of witnesses"* (Hebrews 12:1) who have gone before us, stretching back to those earliest disciples who were called Christians. Like the church at Antioch, the Church of Steel is still poised to **move** the good news of Christ's **love** to the corners of the world. What are you called? Are you prepared to claim the name Christian, to identify your life entirely with Jesus Christ?

Chapter 13

Being Left

Acts 13–14

When Abby and I arrived at our first appointment, in Arlington, Texas, the reality of being corps officers slapped us hard.

1. We were the only people there for Sunday School.

2. One couple decided to see if we would say anything about bringing their dog into the holiness meeting. (We did say something, but only because it got loose during the altar call.)

3. One Sunday, I noticed a very tough looking guy "staring me down" from the back row. After everyone had left, he approached me. Looking me straight in the eye, he said, "Tell me where he is." "Who is *he?*" I asked. "You know … Jack. You need to tell me where Jack is. He works for you and I need to find him."

By this time, I knew our staff well enough to know that we

didn't have a Jack working with us. The man became frustrated. "Listen, I'm a bounty hunter, and I will find Jack." After I lifted my jaw from the floor, I said, "You're a *what?*" "You heard me, I'm a bounty hunter, and you'll be seeing this face every Sunday morning until I find Jack." *Well ... praise the Lord!* I thought. *Now if he would just come to Sunday School, we could have an attendance increase of 50%!*

After those first few weeks in Texas, we sometimes felt like we had **been left** to fend for ourselves in the "Wild West."

Barnabas and Saul (now also called Paul), like Salvation Army officers, had been *"set apart"* in obedience to the Holy Spirit. They were "commissioned" by the church at Antioch; the elders laid hands on them and *"sent them off"* to preach the Gospel. (13:3) They moved from place to place, much as Salvation Army officers do. In each place, they began by proclaiming the Good News in the cities' "corps," the Jewish synagogues. Following this pattern, they evangelized on the island of Cyprus, in Pisidian Antioch (a city with the same name as the one from which they were sent), and in Iconium.

Kicked Out of Two Cities

At Pisidian Antioch, many Jews turned to belief in Jesus when they heard what Paul and Barnabas had to say. The evangelists then had an open door to preach to the whole city, Jews and Gentiles alike, and many Gentiles *"were glad and honored the word of the Lord; and all who were appointed for eternal life believed."* (13:48) But some of the Jewish leaders made trouble for Paul and Barnabas among the *"God–fearing women of high standing and the leading men of the city."* Soon trouble became real persecution, and Paul and Barnabas were expelled. (13:50–51)

In the city of Iconium, once more, they began by preaching in the synagogue, and a *"great number of Jews and Greeks believed."* But again, the Jews who refused to believe *"stirred up the other Gentiles and poisoned their minds against the brothers."* In the face of this opposition, Paul and Barnabas continued to *"speak boldly for the Lord,"* and He enabled them to perform signs and wonders. That is, until they learned of a plot among both the Gentiles and the Jews to *"mistreat and stone them,"* and they were forced to leave town. (14:1–6)

Mistaken for Gods

When the two evangelists arrive in Lystra, they run into a different problem. Paul heals a lame man by the power of the Holy Spirit, and a crowd witnesses it. Instead of listening to the evangelists, the people shout, *"The gods have come down to us in human form!"* (14:8–11)

Knees hit the dirt as people bow down to Paul and Barnabas. They call Barnabas Zeus and Paul, Hermes (the messenger). The local priest of Zeus brings bulls for the crowd to sacrifice to these "gods." As it dawns on Paul and Barnabas that all this is being done for them, I can imagine them looking at each other as if to say, *Boy, these people really aren't getting the message.*

Like leaders trying to get the attention of a hundred unchurched kids at a VBS, Paul and Barnabas do everything they can to wake the people up. They tear their clothes as a sign of disgust at the people's idolatry. No luck.

Faced with a challenge greater than the one we faced with our Arlington bounty hunter, Paul could have felt as though he and Barnabas had **been left** on their own, forging into new territory with this whole "missionary" thing. They had been kicked out of two cities by some very angry people. Now, in Lystra, they have the opposite problem—people who are *too* welcoming, people who think they are gods. The challenge is to try to share the Good News with these idol worshipers who, at this point, totally misunderstand the message. It's possible that Paul felt he had **been left** hanging out to dry.

Not Ready to Give Up

If he did feel that way, his next words to the crowd show that he isn't ready to give up. In a speech that is very similar to his famous address to the crowd at Athens in Acts 17, Paul appeals to the people through natural theology; that is, he shows how the one true God is at work in the natural world around them.

> *'Friends, why are you doing this? We too are only human, like you. We are bringing you good news, telling you to turn from these worthless things to the living God, who made the heavens and the earth and the sea and everything in them. In the past, he let all nations go their own way.* <u>*Yet he has not left himself without testimony*</u>*: He has shown kindness by giving you rain from heaven and crops in their seasons; he provides you with plenty of food and fills your hearts with joy.'* (14:15–17)

When Paul was at the end of his rope with this group in Lystra, he was not **left** alone. The Spirit gave him the words to say. Paul let the crowd know that the one true God had not **left** them either, despite their belief in false gods. *"He has not left himself without testimony,"* Paul proclaims, then shows them how the one true God—not their false gods—manifests his omnipresence and provides for them. The word used here for *testimony* in Greek is *marturon,* from which we get the word *martyr,* which means "witness."

Paul was primarily addressing the pagan culture of Lystra, However, as with all of Scripture, there are broader and deeper implications of this "testimony" or "witness" of the living God. We affirm in The Salvation Army: "We believe that we are justified by grace through faith in our Lord Jesus Christ and that he that believeth hath the witness in himself." (Doctrine 8, taken from 1 John 5:10, *KJV)* The concept of the witness of the Spirit is of prime importance in our understanding of salvation. We believe that the Spirit of God testifies with our spirit that we are children of God. (Romans 8:16) John Wesley, the founder of Methodism, famously had an "Aldersgate moment" when his heart was "strangely warmed." His trust in "Christ alone for my salvation" gave him assurance that Jesus "had taken away my sins, even mine, and saved me from the law of sin and death." That "assurance" was the "witness in himself" that God provided for Wesley. Just as the natural world testifies to the omnipresence of God, the Holy Spirit testifies to the presence of the living God in each of us, His children. As believers in the Lord Jesus, we continue to have the witness in our spirit that we belong to Him. We know that we know that we know. We never need to feel that we have **been left.**

Not Left Alone

Word about what has been going in Lystra on reaches the ears of the Jews in Pisidian Antioch and Iconium who had been against Paul and Barnabas. These troublemakers travel to Lystra to turn the crowd against them. People who honored the evangelists as gods, some of whom have begun to hear and understand their message, now attack Paul. The next thing we know, he has been stoned and left for dead at the edge of town. He is a witness who has almost become a martyr. As blood flows from his body onto the dusty ground, Paul could feel abandoned, **left** hanging out to dry. Then comes a beautiful moment.

> *But after the disciples had gathered around him, he got up and went back into the city.* (14:20)

We learn from this verse that there are *disciples* in Lystra! The ministry of Paul and Barnabas has borne fruit as the Spirit of God has enlightened people's minds to understand the Good News and stirred their hearts to embrace it for themselves. These disciples now gather around Paul, bind his wounds, help him up, and send him on his way. The next day, he and Barnabas move on, to continue their work in another city. We learn that Paul and Barnabas later return to Lystra and the other cities where they were persecuted, *"strengthening the disciples and encouraging them to remain true to the faith."* (14:21–22) So the Word had not fallen on deaf ears!

In our Church of Steel today, as in Lystra, it is the community of believers that surrounds people who are hurting so that they can not only stand up and walk, but get on with the Lord's business. It is through the community that we learn that **God has not left**—that He is providing for all of us through His written Word, through the Holy Spirit, and through the encouragement of other believers.

If you have been knocked down, if you are feeling left out, know that **God has not left,** and He is calling you, through His Holy community, to stand up. He is calling you to stand up and **unite** with Him, to **love** the people in your sphere of influence, and to **move** with His plan. Hopefully we, The Salvation Army, are ready to surround people with the love of Christ when they are down and affirm that not one person should be left. As Salvation Army Doctrine 5 proclaims, "We believe that the Lord Jesus Christ has by His suffering and death made an atonement for the whole world so that whosoever will may be saved." God has not left. He is moving and He will keep moving through the witness of the Holy Spirit.

Are you moving with Him?

Chapter 14
Hold On!

Acts 15

There are few occasions when the word *literally* is used in a correct manner. But I can safely say that, with Acts 15, we have *literally* reached the center of the book. According to Joseph Fitzmyer, an authority on the Greek New Testament, there are 12,385 words in Acts 1–14, and 12,502 words in Acts 15–28. Not only is Acts 15 central in physical placement, but it also represents a crossroads in the New Testament. Without the events and decisions recorded in Acts 15, often referred to as the Jerusalem Council, the Church of Steel likely would have ripped apart; it might even have met its end.

So Acts 15 is the theological and missional center of Luke's narrative. As we have seen, Acts is about the geographical and cultural expansion of the Gospel after Jesus, just before He ascends to the Father, tells the disciples that they *"will be my witnesses in Jerusalem, and in all Judea and Samaria, and to the ends of the earth."* (1:8) The Church takes on that task with the power of the Holy Spirit and then discovers what it means to exist as the Church of Steel, a group of people who **unite, move**, and **love**. But as we come to Acts 15, the Church faces this question: How exactly can we unite when some followers are Jews and some are Gentiles? Certain people's answers to this question threatened to divide and even halt the forward movement of the Church.

Trouble in Antioch

The problem arose in the city of Antioch, where Paul and Barnabas had been winning many Gentiles for Jesus and building a strong church. *"Certain people came down from Judea to Antioch and were teaching the believers: 'Unless you are circumcised, according to the custom taught by Moses, you cannot be saved.' "* (15:1) Paul and Barnabas were suddenly faced with something that could have derailed their plans to move forward. But they said, "Hold on!"

Luke records that they were in *"sharp dispute"* with these people, often called "Judaizers," and began to debate them because they were, in effect, asking Gentiles to become Jews before they could become Christians. The matter was such a sticking point that Paul, Barnabas, and some other believers were sent to the home church in Jerusalem *"to see the apostles and elders about this question."* (15:2) As they traveled, the emissaries from Antioch shared the news about the Gentiles' conversions, and *"This news made all the believers very glad."* (15:3) It's as if Paul and Barnabas were on the campaign trail for the Gentiles!

Holding on to Forms and Signs

Once they arrived in Jerusalem, they came up against a group of believers, members of the *"party of the Pharisees,"* who *"stood up and said, 'The Gentiles must be circumcised and required to keep the law of Moses.'"* (15:5) These believers were adding their own "Hold on!" They were saying, "If we had to follow the law of Moses, then these new converts will have to do it too." They were so committed to their identity as Jews—albeit believers in Jesus—that it was hard for them to imagine that Gentiles wouldn't have to become Jews if they were to become part of the Church.

We too can hold on to forms of Christianity that have shaped us, comforted us, and maybe even brought us closer to God. It might be a church building that was important in our development or a song or hymn sung in a specific style that was meaningful to us. Every denomination has its own idiosyncratic way of operating: Some emphasize baptism; some focus on creeds; some center worship on the Lord's Supper; some revere liturgy.

The denomination in which we serve, The Salvation Army, has a variety of distinctives. The most obvious one is the uniform that soldiers and officers wear. Unfortunately, sometimes we place far too much importance on it. I know a wonderful retired officer, who, when he was in his 80s, said something unfortunate to a soldier. She had decided not to wear her uniform one Sunday. This wonderful, yet in this moment, insensitive, man, said, "Did you leave your salvation at home this morning?" You can imagine the "shock effect" this would have on the soldier.

The uniform is not our salvation, but simply testifies to God's saving grace in our lives. Salvation Army uniforms identify soldiers, make our faith public, and alert people that we are available to them, but uniforms themselves are nothing but tropical wool, silk, and polyester. Our uniforms are symbolic of the work Christ has done in our hearts.

The Pharisees' party, who wanted Gentiles to become circumcised and follow all the rules of Moses, strongly believed that those works were tied up with their salvation. Even though the Gentiles had clearly been won to the Lord Jesus and filled with the Holy Spirit, these believers thought that unless the converts became "like them" as Jews, they couldn't *really* be Christians. The Jewish believers' demands weren't too different from my retired officer friend's equating a Salvation Army uniform with salvation.

This was a crucial moment for the Church of Steel. Could these divergent parties **unite** behind a common vision of how the Christian message was to be expressed and actualized? Were these Gentile believers truly converted, or did they need to follow the Mosaic Law too?

Peter's 'Hold on!'

At this critical juncture, with tensions high, *"The apostles and elders met to consider this question."* (15:6) The "discussion," which no doubt was a heated argument, went on for some time. Then Peter stood up to offer his own "Hold on!" Long before this time, Peter had received a vision from God that made it very clear that as a Jew, he not only could eat with Gentiles but was also called to do so for the sake of the Gospel. He had gone to the house of a centurion named Cornelius and preached the Gospel to him and his household, and they had all received the Holy Spirit. (Acts 10) When Jewish believers criticized his actions, he had to defend them before the leaders at Jerusalem. He argued, *"So if God gave them the same gift he gave us who believed in the Lord Jesus Christ, who was I to think that I could stand in God's way?"* The leaders had to agree with him: *"So then, even to Gentiles God has granted repentance that leads to life."* (11:17–18)

So when Peter stands up to speak at the Jerusalem Council, he reminds the apostles and leaders,

> *'... some time ago, God made a choice among you that the Gentiles might hear from my lips the message of the gospel and believe. God, who knows the heart, showed that he accepted them by giving the Holy Spirit to them, just as he did to us. He did not discriminate between us and them, for he purified their hearts by faith. Now then, why do you try to test God by putting on the necks of Gentiles a yoke that neither we nor our ancestors have been able to bear? No! We believe it is through the grace of our Lord Jesus that we are saved, just as they are.'* (15:8–11)

The Judaizers and the Christian Pharisees insist that laws and traditions have contributed to their salvation. But Peter stops them in their tracks: "Hold on!" He's saying, in effect, "None of us have been able to obey the Law, so why would we put that 'yoke' on the Gentiles? None of us has been saved by the Law." *"No! We believe it is through the grace of our Lord Jesus that we are saved, just as they are."*

The Church of Steel exists when we hold on to this truth—to paraphrase Salvation Army Doctrine #8: We are saved "by grace through faith in our Lord Jesus Christ and they who believe have the witness in themselves." The witness of the Spirit was clearly expressed in the lives of the Gentile believers, who had experienced the justifying grace of God in their lives. This truth centers us and forms us as the Church of Steel:

Jesus' sacrifice, the sole basis of our salvation, is a gift of grace.

When the Church of Steel recognizes how our faith must function, we are no longer dependent upon forms, signs, traditions, or symbols. Instead we are dependent upon the work of the Spirit. He convicts us to repent of our sins and regenerates us, thus making us new people in Christ.

A Momentous Decision

The Council at Jerusalem doesn't end with Peter's speech. *"The whole assembly became silent as they listened to Barnabas and Paul telling about the signs and wonders God had done among the Gentiles through them."* (15:12). After that, James, now the chief elder of the church at Jerusalem, takes the floor. As a Jew Himself, he draws upon the words of the prophet Amos, who spoke of the Lord's return to *"rebuild David's fallen tent ... that the rest of mankind may seek the Lord, even all the Gentiles who bear my name."* (15:16–17)

Then James renders his decision: *"It is my judgment, therefore, that we should not make it difficult for the Gentiles who are turning to God."* He says nothing about circumcision, but states what will be expected of the new believers: They should *"abstain from food polluted by idols, from sexual immorality, from the meat of strangled animals and from blood."* (15:19–20) Those requirements, which were in the Law, would help Jews and Gentiles **unite**. The leaders of the Jerusalem church affirm this decision with a letter, which also acknowledges that *"some went out from us without our authorization and disturbed you, troubling your minds by what they said"* (15:24)—in effect, rebuking those who have taught that Gentiles needed to become Jews to become Christians.

When the believers in Antioch received the letter, they "were glad for its encouraging message." (15:31) They didn't see the requirements of the Council as burdensome. But imagine what the reaction would have been if the letter had said the work of the Spirit in their lives wasn't enough—that they would have to be circumcised to be a part of the Kingdom!

Without the pivotal "Hold on!" of Acts 15, we wouldn't have a Church of Steel today. This was a climactic event, *literally* at the center of Acts, when the Church made a conscious decision to **unite** under the banner of grace, making it possible to bring the good news about Jesus to the *"ends of the earth."* Instead of holding onto a form of religion, the Church of Steel joined—together, Jews and Gentiles alike—in the movement of God.

Are there ways that we in the Church today are holding back that movement? If there are, it's time for us to say, "Hold on!"

Chapter 15

'We' Is Way
Better than 'They'

Acts 16:10

Social media is a blessing and a curse. It's a blessing because we can stay in touch with a wide circle of family and friends. But occasionally I find it hard to see people enjoying beautiful scenery, picture–perfect moments, and delicious foods. (Seriously, folks, can we please stop taking pictures of our food?) There have been times when several friends have been at the same conference or concert, and their social media posts have reminded me that I simply was not there. Through their eyes, I can see what happened, but I am a mere observer. Watching but not participating is hard.

You may feel at this point as if you are a "watcher" and not a participant in the book of Acts. You may feel that the story is about things that really happened, but it doesn't necessarily involve you. You may be thinking, *I might as well be reading a history book about the Civil War.*

That feeling could come from the way the first part of Acts is written, in the third person, which gives us an objective, "bird's-eye" view. Acts 16 begins in the same vein as we read about Paul's missionary travels. In 16:6, we read that *"Paul and his companions traveled throughout the region of Phrygia and Galatia, having been kept by the Holy Spirit from preaching the word in the province of Asia."* You might be thinking, *Here we go again. Another story about this church unrelated to me.*

Circle This in Your Bible!

Then there's a subtle literary shift. It's a significant change, one so "under the radar" that it's easy to miss. I remember when I first learned about this shift in Luke's writing. I wondered how I had missed such a small but important change. Here Luke is no longer talking about the events as a bystander or witness. No longer is he simply describing the journey of this Church of Steel throughout *"Jerusalem, Judea, Samaria, and to the ends of the earth"* in an objective way. Luke writes, *" ... we got ready at once to leave for Macedonia ... "* (16:10) Did you catch that? He's using the first person plural, **we**. He's including himself in the story! In most of the rest of Acts, he describes events this way. The story is no longer just about what is happening to other people; instead, it's about what Luke experienced too.

Why has Luke shifted from third person to first person? Why is he now talking about "we" instead of "they"? He has made the change because he's no longer just an observer but part of the team.

Some have suggested that this change to "we" may be an error on the part of the editors of the book of Acts. To that, I say,

"Hogwash!" Luke is a careful writer. The person who catalogued what happened from Jesus' birth to His death, the person who recorded exactly what happened on the day of Pentecost, would know exactly what he was doing when he made that abrupt shift to "we."

Therefore, we may confidently infer that this is the point at which the writer of Acts joins in the action. This shift is something worth underlining or circling in your Bible. In the verses just before 16:10, Luke was still referring to the work in the third person, " ... *the Spirit of Jesus would not allow* them *to ... [enter Bithynia]. So* they *passed by Mysia and went down to Troas. During the night Paul had a vision of a man of Macedonia standing and begging him, 'Come over to Macedonia and help us.' "* (16:8–9) (Macedonia refers to the region where Philippi and Thessalonica are located. Paul would later write letters to the churches he and his companions planted in this region—one to the Philippians and two to the Thessalonians.)

Christian tradition and a later source in the New Testament tell us that Luke was a physician. F.F. Bruce, a highly respected New Testament scholar, speculates that if Luke is the physician Paul mentions in Colossians 4:4, " ... we may wonder if [Luke] was practicing his profession in Troas at the time [Paul arrived], or waiting to be signed on as a ship's doctor." We have no way of knowing. But what we do know is that for whatever reason, Luke decided to join Paul on his journey. That's shown in our key verse, 16:10: *"After Paul had seen the vision,* we *got ready at once to leave for Macedonia, concluding that God had called* us *to preach the gospel to them."* The team, now including Luke, "got ready *at once*" to advance together for what God was calling them to do.

We Can't Be Bystanders

Just as Luke is no longer a bystander to the action, neither can we be bystanders. Just as Paul had a vision of a man standing and begging him to come, we must *"conclude"* that we have to join together because *" ... God has called us to preach the gospel to them."*

Notice that the text does not say God has called only those with the gift of evangelism *"to preach the gospel to them."* It does not say only those with self-assurance should *"preach the gospel to them."* Nor does it say that Luke plans to go it alone. He's not speaking in the first person singular. He is not saying, *"I* felt the need to preach the gospel." Instead, he is saying that God called *"us to preach the gospel to them."*

My kids watch a show on PBS Kids called "Super Why." Each show revolves around a classic story chosen from the library. Super Reader characters jump into the story, sharing in the experiences of Robin Hood, Cinderella, and a variety of other famous characters from fairy tales and legends. When we become followers of Christ, we too get to jump into and live out the story of God's saving plan. We get to share in the life of Jesus. We have the opportunity to share in the Gospel, to jump into the story of God's work where we live. The hope of the world comes through the Church of Jesus Christ that is on the **move,** that is **united**, that **loves** in Jesus' name.

I am thankful for some short YouTube videos that have educated me about being a handyman in our house. From such a video, I learned how to unclog a drain in a bathroom. After I did this task, I was so impressed with myself that I enjoyed watching the water flow for a while. But when I was putting my sink back together, I realized that a part was missing. There's this one little piece of metal, not more than two inches long, that connects the drain to a little stick that stops the drain. And I could not find that little piece anywhere. I went to the hardware store and tried to describe the part, but my vocabulary lacked the detail I needed. The guys there took 15 minutes trying to understand me. Finally they said, "Oh! You mean a wing nut!" I said, "If you say so!" Sure enough, that's what I needed. It wasn't until I purchased and installed this crazy little 49–cent piece of metal that my job was complete.

All the pieces must come together for a job to be complete. And all the people of our congregations must come together for the Church of Steel to be realized where we live. We must come to the same place as Luke in the writing of Acts. We cannot be satisfied with describing what other people have done in the past. We cannot be satisfied with sitting in the bleachers and observing the work of the church. We cannot be satisfied with financially supporting the work of the church and doing nothing else. Instead we must participate in the story; we must see the story as about "we" and not "they."

You and I are part of the **we** that is the branch of the Christian Church known as The Salvation Army. We believe we are in a fight against sin and its effects in our world. We believe that we need to slay some dragons in Jesus' name, that we need to have the holy courage to fight against sin and to bring people to a place of knowing Jesus, of knowing the adventure He has in store for us.

"We" is better than "they"; "we" is also better than "I." Jesus thought so, and demonstrated it by what He did. His incarnation, His life, His death, His resurrection, and His ascension happened so that **we** could join Him in a new creation of the world.

When I think about the choruses and songs in the *Salvation Army Song Book* that I normally choose for times of meditation and altar calls, I realize that most of them are in the first person singular: "*I* surrender all"; "All there is of *me,* Lord"; "It's no longer *I* that liveth"; "All *my* days and all *my* hours." But many of the "warfare" songs and choruses are in the first person plural. The concept of an Army is a shared journey. There cannot be an Army of one. There can only be an Army of many people joined in a task together. Together, **we** "Join the fight for the right, in His everlasting might, and sing **our** marching song." *(SASB,* #932) That joyful march will take **us** from this life into eternity.

We'll sing in the morning the songs of salvation,

We'll sing in the noontide the songs of His love,

And when we arrive at the end of our journey

We'll sing the songs of Zion in the courts above.

SASB, #555

Chapter 16

Play the Rests

Acts 16:1–31

As a music major, I was never the first chair trumpet player; in orchestra, I generally played second or third chair. When a composition didn't have a second or third trumpet part, I became a "utility player." One time, that meant I was a temporary percussionist assigned to the *grancassa*, which is Italian for bass drum.

This assignment gave me the opportunity of getting to know the principal percussionist, an attractive young lady named Abby. This was just the start of my romance with my future wife. Though it took several more months for me to get her attention, I thank the Lord for my days playing the *grancassa!*

As a percussionist, there were times when I did not have a part to play, and I became familiar with a word that is some-times written across percussion parts: *tacet*. It means "silent." The players are following the score, but their instruments need to be silent. For the percussionists, these are "rests." They are temporarily sidelined.

Sometimes, in our own lives, we have to work through times or difficulties that suddenly seem to put us on the sidelines, to make us seemingly unimportant or insignificant.

Sidelined—to Jail

In Philippi, where Paul and Silas had **moved** with the Spirit into a new mission field, they were troubled by a fortune-telling slave girl, possessed by an evil spirit, who kept shouting at them. After "many days" of dealing with this situation, Paul miraculously cast the evil spirit from her. Her owners—who lost a major source of income from the girl's fortune telling—became so furious that they *"seized Paul and Silas and dragged them into the marketplace to face the authorities."* Egged on by an angry crowd, the magistrates had Paul and Silas stripped and beaten. Then Paul and Silas were thrown into the "inner cell" of the jail with their feet fastened to the floor in stocks. (16:16–24)

As a result of being **united** with God's plan, Paul and Silas were suddenly sidelined from their mission. The slave girl's owners, the crowd, and the magistrates had "benched" them from their work of spreading the Gospel. Or at least that's what it looked like.

Few of us will ever be physically persecuted and jailed like Paul and Silas as we work for the Lord. But we might encounter opposition or face a physical illness that seems to put us on the sidelines. Or we might enter a new phase of life and feel as if we've been benched. But it would be a mistake to think that God has done that. We have to remember that He is the master of every situation we face. A proper understanding of His providence should lead us to affirm His sovereignty—not just over the universe, but over every circumstance of our lives. One prominent theologian has a specific way of casting this truth: "God may not be the author of every situation, but he is the master of every situation." In musical terms, we're the players, and God is the Conductor.

Paul and Silas, while chained and imprisoned, could have easily shaken their fists at God, saying, "This isn't fair! We could do so much more without these chains!" But they didn't do that. They knew that God has a way of mastering challenges, even one as tough as this one.

Just as I was taught, as a percussionist, to play the *tacet* part as a rest, Paul and Silas were in a position where their mission in Philippi was still active, but silent.

My grandfather had the unique privilege of being the official chauffeur for two famous musicians, Erik Leidzen and Eric Ball, arguably the greatest Salvation Army composers of the 20th century. Eric Ball would occasionally visit Leidzen when he traveled to New York City, and my grandfather would be called upon to drive them around. He said it was tedious at times, but he enjoyed listening to their conversations. One time, Leidzen asked him to stop the car. He pointed his finger at my grandpa and chided him (with a strong Swedish accent): "The problem with you preachers is you don't know how to play the rests. If you are to be an effective preacher, young Miller, you must learn to play the rests. Every composer knows that silence and rest is a necessary part of the music that must be played. You preachers never break long enough for us to think about what you are saying. Miller, learn to play the rests." My grandfather took this message to heart and incorporated silence (rests) into his preaching from that day forward.

The Time for Silence Ends

Playing the rests for Paul and Silas meant **uniting** with God's mission even when they were in a challenging place. It would seem that being jailed had taken them out of the action. But they stayed connected with the Conductor of their lives and did something with their time on the sidelines—they played the rests.

Then suddenly, the time for silence was over: *"About midnight Paul and Silas were praying and singing hymns to God, and the other prisoners were listening to them."* (16:25)

As they were singing, an earthquake struck and the prison doors flew open. The jailer, who had been asleep, awoke to see the situation, and he *"was about to kill himself because he thought the prisoners had escaped."* But Paul stopped him from falling on his sword. He cried, *"Don't harm yourself! We are all here!"* We understand why Paul and Silas would stay, but why did the other prisoners stay? Perhaps it was because of what they heard as Paul and Silas prayed and sang. The fact that the two missionaries stayed in the jail also gave them the opportunity to **love** the jailer into the Kingdom and win his entire household. (16:26–34)

We may not feel that we have the strength to play the rests in our lives. We may not feel we have the strength to deal with a difficult child, to keep working in a challenging vocation, to be faithful when challenges come. You might be thinking, "I could never be like Paul and Silas." But remember that Paul and Silas didn't play the rests because of any strength they had in themselves. The Holy Spirit gave Paul and Silas the grace to accept apparently being put on the sidelines, and then to sing when they seemingly had no reason to sing. And God gives us the grace to play the rests too, to serve Him even during tough times. Remember, He is the master of every circumstance in our lives.

Trials, and the reality that we will have times when we will be called upon to "play the rests," shouldn't cause us to doubt the reality of God's presence and God's direction in our lives. He will be with us and give us the grace to play those rests as we **move** with His mission, **love** people in His strength, and **unite** with His Spirit.

Part Three
Stay the Course

Chapter 17

Facing Opposition

Acts 17:1–15

So far in our study of Acts, we have looked at how important it is to **take our place** in the action of God's movement in the world. Then we began to understand how that action shapes a Church of Steel that **unites, moves,** and **loves.** Now we approach the latter part of Acts, which teaches us how we must **stay the course** if we are to continue to be a part of the great movement of God in the future.

Luke's unfolding of the expansion of the Gospel began with Jesus' ascension in Chapter 1 of Acts. Just before He departed, Jesus set the direction for His followers: " *... you will be my witnesses in Jerusalem, and in all Judea and Samaria, and to the ends of the earth."* (1:8) This geographic expansion is what makes up the "stuff" of Acts. Luke's primary focus is on the way God works through Jesus by the Spirit on behalf of the people of "the Way"—now known as Christians—as they spread the Gospel throughout the known world.

The Apostle Paul becomes a leading character in the story Luke tells in Acts. We learn that in Troas, Luke joined Paul on his missionary journeys, which would eventually take Paul to Rome. But the mission was far from smooth sailing. In Philippi, when Paul and Silas were flogged and jailed for preaching the Gospel, they were sidelined and seemingly derailed. Yet they **stayed the course**, and the glorious result was that a jailer and his household were won for the Kingdom. (16:16–34)

As we come to Acts 17, we find Paul and Silas in a new city, Thessalonica. Paul was called by Jesus to be the apostle to the Gentiles. (Romans 11:13) But wherever he went, if there was a synagogue in town, he started his ministry there. He preached the Gospel first to the Jews, the people who were looking for the Messiah, the people who knew what the Scriptures prophesied about Him. So, in Thessalonica, Paul goes to the synagogue three Sabbaths in a row to reason with the Jews, proving to them from Scripture, *"This Jesus I am proclaiming to you is the Messiah."* (17:1–3)

Here, we get an inside look at how Paul proclaimed the Gospel in the synagogue. He *"reasoned"* with his hearers, *"explaining and proving that the Messiah had to suffer and rise from the dead."* (17:2–3) His presentation is intellectually focused because he is speaking to people who know the Scriptures well. He doesn't play upon their emotions. Instead, he uses a simple "if–then" form of rhetoric. The logic is:

If A is true: The Messiah must suffer and rise again as proven by Scriptures;

And B is true: Jesus suffered and died and was resurrected—and I saw Him, as did many others;

Then C must be true: Jesus is the Messiah.

Then Comes the 'But'

The response to Paul's message, as in other cities, is at first positive: *"Some of the Jews were persuaded and joined Paul and Silas, as did a large number of God–fearing Greeks and quite a few prominent women."* (17:4)

Then Luke signals that all is not well by beginning the next paragraph with the word *but*. *"But other Jews were jealous; so they rounded up some bad characters from the marketplace, formed a mob and started a riot in the city."* The mob started a mad search for Paul and Silas so that they could bring them before the local authorities. Next comes a scene in which men are attacked and dragged out into the streets. (17:5–6)

Because this same type of scene happens often in Acts, my brain sometimes goes on auto–pilot and assumes it's Paul who has been attacked. But it's not. It's a man named Jason. The mob rushed to Jason's house, and when they didn't find Paul and Silas there, they dragged Jason and other believers who were with him before the city officials.

Who is this Jason? Obviously, he must be associated in people's minds with Paul and Silas. Paul, in his first letter to the church in Thessalonica, writes that he worked at his trade as a tentmaker so that he would not have to be supported by the believers in that city. New Testament scholar Ben Witherington suggests that Jason could have been a business partner who came to Christ and worked with Paul. In any case, we know that Jason has entertained Paul and Silas in his home. The crowd shouts the charge: *"These men [Paul and Silas] who have caused trouble all over the world have now come here, and Jason has welcomed them into his house. They are all defying Caesar's decrees, saying that there is another king, one called Jesus."* (17:6–7)

The charge, which puts the cause of Jesus (and by extension, the cause of Paul and Silas) in direct opposition to Roman rule, throws the gathered crowd and the city officials into turmoil. They let Jason and the other believers go, but not before they post bond, which means the case against them is far from over. Paul and Silas are forced to leave under cloak of darkness. *"As soon as it was night, the believers sent [them] away to Berea."* (17:8–10) The two evangelists have been accused of causing trouble all over the world—translated in many Bible versions as "turning the world upside down"—but they might have felt, at that moment, that the world was turning against the Gospel.

The Pattern Repeats Itself

The same pattern repeats itself at Berea. Paul and Silas go to the synagogue, preaching the Good News about Jesus as Messiah. They meet with even greater success here than at Thessalonica. The Berean Jews *"received the message with great eagerness and examined the Scriptures every day to see if what Paul said was true. As a result, many of them believed, as did also a number of prominent Greek women and many Greek men."* (17:11–12)

Then comes the *but*. *"But when the Jews in Thessalonica learned that Paul was preaching the word of God at Berea, some of them went there too, agitating the crowds and stirring them up. The believers immediately sent Paul to the coast ... "* (17:13)

Once again, as they were "turning the world upside down," the world seemed to turn against Paul and Silas. They could very well have felt discouraged. But they were partners in the Gospel and could encourage one another, and that made it easier to **stay the course.** Because many had believed, despite the opposition, they also knew that God was at work.

In these stories, it's not just the main actors who stay the course. It's the whole team, including the newest believers.

Fierce Commitment

Every four years, the soccer World Cup captures the attention and intrigue of people around the globe. Even if you don't enjoy soccer or know very little about it, you have to admire the way the players stay focused. Though the scoreboard might tally very few goals—sometimes, none at all—the players continue to run with fierce intention so that when the ideal moment comes to score a goal, they can be in position to strike. That takes focus and commitment.

Paul and Silas had such commitment. Despite opposition at every turn, they kept proclaiming the Gospel. Jason and the others with him had such commitment. They were willing to take the heat for Paul and Silas. The new believers at Thessalonica had such commitment. Under cover of darkness, and presumably in the face of great danger, they spirited Paul and Silas away to Berea. When opposition arose there, the believers had such commitment. Despite possible dire consequences, they made sure Paul got away safely.

In both Thessalonica and Berea, unnamed believers, tuned in to the mission that the Gospel must reach *"the ends of the earth,"* helped Paul and Silas to **stay the course.** Because these unnamed believers faithfully performed their task, they ensured that the Gospel would continue to be proclaimed.

There are thousands, if not millions, of believers whose names will never be recorded in books outlining the history of the Church. And there are people reading these pages who are unheralded and unnoticed as they work to advance the Kingdom. These "supporting players," though unrecognized, are essential in enabling everyone to **stay the course.**

Unnamed but Essential

Maybe you are one of those supporting players. Maybe you faithfully sign a check in support of the work of The Salvation Army. Maybe you are faithful in prayer for your leaders and gladly lift burdens from them. Maybe you are subtly building a friendship with a neighbor or colleague who is not a Christian. Even though your role may not be public, you are taking your place in God's redemptive story.

Paul, Silas, Jason, and many unnamed believers in the stories about the mission in Thessalonica and Berea saw their plans subverted, but they also took action, as the Spirit led them, to ensure that God's plan would prevail. We also will sometimes face opposition that can hold back or even temporarily derail our mission. Despite what it looks like at any given moment, we must have faith that God's plan will prevail. Our job is to be faithful in our task, as the Spirit leads us, to **stay the course** so that the Gospel will be proclaimed where we live and to the ends of the earth.

Often in The Salvation Army, we end big meetings with a great song: "I'll Go in the Strength of the Lord." *(SASB* #959) My father–in–law, a Methodist minister, first sang that song while visiting a Salvation Army event. His comment was, "Well, now I am ready to run through a brick wall for Jesus!"

Recently I was arrested by the last line of the last verse. I had sung it, as I usually do, with robust confidence. But immediately afterward, I was struck by the power of these six words: "to suffer and triumph I'll go!" Paul, the Thessalonian Christians, and the Berean Christians all knew that they would likely have to suffer before they could triumph. But they were faithful to **stay the course** anyway. Are we so committed? Are we willing to suffer to see the Kingdom expanded?

We don't know how God will initiate a move in His Church today. But we do know that God wants to bring people to know Jesus through His Spirit. We know that *"the Lord Jesus Christ has by his suffering and death made an atonement for the whole world so that whosoever will may be saved."* (Salvation Army doctrine #6) When the world turns against us, we must continue to trust that God will triumph through His holy love. Our business is to turn the world upside down so that people will be saved and God's plan will advance. It's worth any struggle to **stay the course** because we get to be a part of God's redemptive story as He fulfills the Scriptures and ushers in the second coming of Jesus, the King of Kings.

Chapter 18

What Do You Mean?

Acts 17:14–34

I'm sure you've heard the old adage, "Say what you mean, and mean what you say." The first part of it strikes at the nature of intention; that is, what we really mean when we say particular things. Our 4–year–old daughter, Georgia, has started verbalizing about her spiritual life. Recently she took great care to tell us about what she does when she prays. She gave us a step–by–step description, "First I go into my room and close the door. Then I go to my bed and turn around. Then I get my knees on and I pray to Jesus." Now of course, Georgia doesn't really put her knees *on*. What she really means is that she gets *on* her knees. (Though I do like her way of putting it; I think we all need to be people who get our "knees on.") We understood Georgia's intention even if her words were not perfectly clear. We got her meaning.

In the famous speech that the Apostle Paul gives in Athens,

121

he has a clear opportunity to witness to unbelievers, to "say what he means and mean what he says." As the scene in Acts 17 opens, some philosophers hear Paul presenting the Good News, and they ask, in effect, "What do you mean?" As Paul answers, he unfolds the deep implications of their question and tries to show the philosophers what *they* mean to the one true God.

Paul found himself alone in Athens, waiting for Timothy and Silas to join him. But he could not remain idle because he became *"greatly distressed to see that the city was full of idols."* So, as in other cities, he first *"reasoned in the synagogue with both Jews and God-fearing Greeks."* Then he took his message into the marketplace, which had also become a "marketplace of ideas." As Luke tells us, *"All the Athenians and foreigners who lived [in Athens] spent their time doing nothing but talking about and listening to the latest ideas."* Paul's "reasoning" catches the attention of some Epicurean and Stoic philosophers, who begin to debate with him. They call him a *"babbler"* who *"seems to be advocating foreign gods."* (17:14–18a, 21)

Luke tells us, *"They said this because Paul was preaching the good news about Jesus <u>and</u> the resurrection."* Most commentators suggest that the philosophers could very easily have thought that when Paul talked about the resurrection (*anastasis*), he was talking about a different god besides Jesus. Intrigued by what Paul has been saying, the philosophers bring him to the famous Areopagus (Mars Hill) Council—you might call it the Supreme Court of Athens—to defend his ideas. They begin by asking, *"May we know what this new teaching is that you are presenting? You are bringing some strange ideas to our ears, and we would like to know what they mean."* The philosophers are asking for the meaning of what Paul has said. He is about to offer them instead the fulfillment of the desire of every human heart: the meaning of life. (17:18b–20)

As Paul is given the floor, he begins by challenging his listeners, essentially flipping the question to ask, "What do these idols of yours mean?" He says, *"People of Athens! I see that in every way you are very religious."* (17:22) Paul is "buttering up" the crowd—complimenting them on their spirituality—before challenging their pluralistic ways. We might not think of our world as pluralistic—having many gods. But how often have you heard people say things like, "There's truth in every religion, so I can believe in Buddha and karma and Jesus all at the same time"? The problem is that when you believe in everything, you end up believing in nothing.

The Athenians wanted to cover all their bases, so, in addition to all the gods they "knew," they had *"an altar with this inscription: TO AN UNKNOWN GOD."* Paul jumps at the opportunity to "fill the gap" for them: *"So you are ignorant of the very thing you worship—and this is what I am going to proclaim to you."* (17:23–24) Paul has been brought to court to explain what *he* means, but he is about to turn the tables and let the people of Athens know how *they* can find meaning—through knowing the one true God.

When my wife's family gets together, they often tell a story about Abby's brother, Will. The story goes that my father–in–law was painting his office at the church. Will, then 3 or 4 years old, got into the paint and made a mess. When my father–in–law came in, he said in frustration, "Will, why did you get into the paint!?" And Will, without blinking an eye, said, "Dad, why do men climb mountains?" Will turned the question around, making the point that it's just as hard to find meaning for why men climb mountains as it is to find meaning in why kids make messes. But Paul didn't use his turn–it–around moment to get himself out of trouble. He used his rhetorical skills to help his listeners understand how they could find true meaning in their lives.

In the middle of an intellectual battle with the elite thinkers of his day, Paul **stays the course**, laying the Gospel out before them, showing them the road to salvation. But there were some potholes on that road for the people of Athens. We need to avoid those potholes—and help others avoid them—if we are to **stay the course** with God.

Pothole #1. The Athenians believed their gods could be confined.

For them, worship was directed toward objects—idols and the temples they built for them. But the one true God is not made of clay or stone, and He isn't bound by church walls. As Paul put it, *"The God who made the world and everything in it is the Lord of heaven and earth and does not live in temples built by human hands."* (17:24) True meaning comes from faith in the Lord of all creation, who cannot be confined to a building or even by our expectations of Him.

As a boy, I grew up hearing my dad preach. He had phrases he would often use, such as, "The altar is now open." One Sunday evening I resisted going to the altar and after the benediction, I left the chapel in tears. My mom found me in a corner crying. She asked me what was wrong, and I said, "Mom, the altar is closed, and I missed my chance." I had taken my dad's statement literally. I figured if the altar could be opened, then at some point in time, it must be closed, as if there were a force field that came over those pieces of wood to open and close them like department–store doors.

God is not restricted to altars—or chapels or camps or perceptions or roles or any other of the boxes we put around Him. When God came to Moses in the burning bush, Moses asked what God's name was, so he could tell the people. God said simply, *"I am who I am."* (Exodus 3:14) This statement speaks of God's nature and how He exists outside our projections of him. If we are to **stay the course,** we must know that we cannot—and should not—restrict God. When we allow the Lord of the universe to have full sway in our lives, He will provide us with the understanding and the power to **stay the course.**

Pothole #2. The Athenians believed there were many gods and that every one of them had to be worshiped.

The so–called "religious" people of Athens thought it was essential that they worship and serve every god in the world. Paul challenges that idea with a truth that must have been startling to his audience:

> 'The God who made the world and everything in it is the Lord of heaven and earth and does not live in temples built by human hands. And he is not served by human hands, as if he needed anything. Rather, he himself gives everyone life and breath and everything else.' (17:24–25)

If the Athenians could just once look to the source of "*life and breath and everything else,*" Paul is saying, they would find out what *they themselves* mean within the grand scheme of the universe. So Paul answers the question, "What do you mean?" by telling his listeners about the one (and only) God who created everything that exists and gives us life.

A prolific British New Testament scholar, I. Howard Marshall, points out that the Greek word for *life* in this passage is *zōē,* which was popularly associated with the supreme Greek god, Zeus. Marshall writes that when Paul uses the triadic phrase, "*'life and breath and everything else,'*" he is saying, "God is the source of life; Zeus isn't.'"[1]

---

1   I. Howard Marshall, *Acts: Tyndale New Testament Commentaries* (Westmont, IL: IVP Academic, 2008).

We may think we are far superior to the Athenians because we don't worship multiple gods. But we can create our own "gods"—sports or entertainment idols, political figures, the "toys" in our lives, material success, even our own spouses or children—and attempt to derive meaning from these things. To put anyone or anything above God is idolatry just as surely as worshiping before a statue of Zeus is idolatry. If we are to **stay the course,** we must not fall prey to worshiping false gods. They will inevitably fail us, but our God never does.

Pothole #3. The philosophers believed in gods who were not involved in people's lives.

The Stoics acknowledged a creator of sorts, but they thought he was unconcerned with people and far from their reality. The Epicureans also taught that the gods had no interest in human lives. I believe many people have this kind of image of God, as some far–off being "in a galaxy far, far away." Sure, these people would tell you, God created the Earth, but then He left it alone and has no concern for what is happening in it now. But that's not the God we know. Paul explains to the Athenians what He is like:

> 'From one man he made all the nations, that they should inhabit the whole earth; and he marked out their appointed times in history and the boundaries of their lands. God did this so that they would seek him and perhaps reach out for him and find him, though he is not far from any of us.' (17:26–27)

Paul is saying that God is in control, and He is never far away from us! He is here; He is close; and He wants us to reach out to Him. That's a message of hope for the world. Our real significance, our true meaning, comes as we recognize that *"in him we live and move and have our being."* (17:28)

If "we are God's offspring," as Paul reasons, then the divine being cannot be *"like silver or gold or stone—an image made by human design and skill."* Once upon a time, Paul says, God overlooked the ignorance of people who believed that, but the time has now come for *"all peoples everywhere to repent."* He finishes his argument by saying that a day of judgment is coming, and *"the man he has appointed"* will be in charge. Paul doesn't name that man, but he says God has given proof of who He is by raising Him from the dead. (17:29–31)

Paul **stayed the course** in communicating truth to his audience. Some of them rejected it outright—they actually sneered. A number of them believed—including Dionysius (a member of the Areopagus) and a woman named Damaris. But others said, *"We want to hear you again on this subject."* (17:32–34) They believed they had time to keep debating.

I'm sure Paul was discouraged by such a response. We've all been there as we've witnessed to people who think they have all the time in the world to make a decision for Jesus. It's up to us to **stay the course,** not in our own strength but because we are connected to the one who was raised from the dead.

After all, Jesus, through his life, death, and victorious resurrection **stayed the course** for us. The reality of His resurrection is the beginning of the new creation, the sign of promise that the chaotic nature of the world can have meaning. So we must persist, as Jesus persisted for us, so that more people can discover what *they* mean in God's big story.

Chapter 19

Connected

Acts 18:1–11

As Acts 18 opens, Paul has left Athens, presumably alone. His mission there had met with limited success, with only "some" people in the pagan city turning to belief in Jesus. So as he arrives in Corinth, still alone, it's possible he's feeling somewhat disheartened. Then he meets a couple who will play an important role in New Testament history. Priscilla and Aquila, like Paul, have arrived in Corinth under difficult circumstances. In 49 A.D., Emperor Claudius had exiled them—along with all Jews—from Rome.

So Aquila and Priscilla—and, sometime later, Paul—arrived in Corinth, unconnected and likely feeling defeated. But very quickly, they found one another. Priscilla and Aquila had evidently become followers of the Way while they were in Rome. When Paul learned that they were in Corinth, he went to see them. Aquila and Priscilla were in the tentmaking business, and that was Paul's trade as well, so they worked together. (18:2–3) They also likely supported one another in the mission. When Paul later wrote to the Roman believers (about A.D. 56–57), he had not been to that city himself, but he asked the believers there to *"Greet Priscilla and Aquila, my co–workers in Christ"*— who, by that time, had returned to Rome. Paul wrote that the couple *"risked their lives for me. Not only I but all the churches of the Gentiles are grateful to them."* (Romans 16:3–4)

One of those Gentile churches started in Corinth. Two hundred years earlier, the city had been destroyed by the Romans, but in 44 B.C., Julius Caesar decided to make it a retirement city for the military. So, with significant backing from Rome, the town got a facelift and became firmly established. A port city, it was a regional hub for economic development. This was a town that was "up–and–coming."

Corinth had also become a "sin city." Darrell Bock, a New Testament scholar, calls Corinth the Las Vegas of its time.[1] Gordon Fee says it was like a combination of New York (financial capital), Las Vegas (debauchery capital) and Los Angeles (entertainment capital).[2]

Every two years, Corinth hosted the Isthmian Games, a significant sporting and cultural event that drew tens of thousands of tourists. Today, cities covet being named to host events like the World Cup, the Super Bowl, or the Olympics just one time. But imagine the economic boon it would be for a city to host the

---

1   Bock, *Acts*.

2   Gordon D. Fee has led many translations of the New Testament and is seen as a dean of the study of the Corinthian letters. This comparison in mentioned in his and Douglas Stuart's book *How to Read the Bible for All Its Worth* (Grand Rapids: Zondervan, 2003).

Olympics every other year.[3] The games created a huge demand for tents—and a lot of work for Priscilla, Aquila, and Paul. They also would have been able to make a missional connection to people seeking lodging as they came to Corinth. Then, when the work week ended, *"Every Sabbath [Paul] reasoned in the synagogue, trying to persuade Jews and Greeks."* (18:4)

The Team Comes Together

When Silas and Timothy arrive from Macedonia, they bring Paul a gift of money from the churches there, so he no longer has to work to earn a living. (2 Corinthians 11:9) That means he doesn't have to confine his preaching to the Sabbath, but can devote himself *"exclusively to preaching, testifying to the Jews that Jesus was Messiah."* (18:5) And Paul is **connected** to a team that now includes Priscilla, Aquila, Silas, and Timothy. Paul is able to do what he does because of the support he has— and because he's following God's plan, His agenda.

I've sometimes been upset that God doesn't follow my agenda. This can be difficult for me, at times, because I think I have a good agenda. I have a solid plan backed up by research, experience, and most importantly, what will make me happy. I sometimes feel it would be much easier for me if God would simply follow the course I have laid out for Him. But I'm not called to follow my own agenda. Paul wasn't called to do that either. His call—and my call, and your call—is to seek out God's will, follow it, and **stay the course** even when opposition comes.

When Paul began preaching in Corinth, he first did as he had done in other cities: he brought the word that Jesus is the

---

3   When Paul writes to the Corinthians, he uses this "game" analogy: *"Do you not know that in the race all runners run, but only one gets the prize? Run in such a way as to get the prize."* (1 Corinthians 9:24).

long–promised Messiah to the Jews and God–fearing Greeks in the synagogue. *"But when they opposed Paul and became abusive, he shook out his clothes in protest and said to them, 'Your blood be on your own heads! I am innocent of it. From now on I will go to the Gentiles.'"* (18:6) Paul was rejected by his own people, but he was able to **stay the course** because of his connections—to his team and to His Lord.

Together, We Win

My grandfather, whose name I share, was described by some people of his time as the best–known Salvationist in America. Since his promotion to Glory, I sometimes have viewed his legacy through rose–colored glasses. But every now and then, it's helpful for me to remember that he took hard stands that didn't always make him popular. I remember him saying to me,

> You know, Ange, there are people who don't like me. They would be just as glad if I took off this uniform and pumped gas. And I have to admit that I can't do much for them. And that's OK. It was a great relief to me when I realized that I didn't have to win the world for Jesus by myself. I've been made as a unique person. Some people, Ange, don't like me because I am loud, because I am from New York, or because I like to go for this team or that. Some people don't like me because of my father.

Softly tapping his index finger on my chest, he slowly spoke the next words directly into my life, "Ange, you've got to know this fact. People won't like you either, but you get yours and I'll get mine ... and together we'll win the world for Jesus."

I have treasured these words from my grandfather, "Together

we will win the world for Jesus," as I think about my calling in life. It is **together** that we can accomplish God's purposes for our towns, for our corps. Paul realized this. He realized he needed to be a part of a community, a part of a team, a part of a support system that could strategize and use their collective gifts for the Kingdom. God has called us to be more than we are by ourselves. **Together** we will win the world for Jesus; **together** we will see who God has called us to be; **together** we can stay the course. We can say this with confidence because Jesus has already won the victory on the Cross. He **stayed the course** as the author and perfecter of our faith through the power of the Holy Spirit. It is that same Holy Spirit we depend on today; it is that same Holy Spirit who enables us as a community to **stay the course** and move "forward to the fight."

Connected to Jesus—and Mission

Paul's confidence was based on much more than his connection to his colleagues; it was based most importantly on his connection to Jesus and the Holy Spirit. After his bad experience, Paul moves on and continues to preach His message of hope to the Gentiles. Many believe and are baptized; even a Jew named Crispus, the synagogue leader, turns to the Lord, along with his entire household. It is in this context, when Paul is following God's agenda, that he hears directly from Jesus. *"One night the Lord spoke to Paul in a vision: 'Do not be afraid; keep on speaking, do not be silent. For I am with you, and no one is going to attack and harm you, because I have many people in this city.' "* (18:7–10)

"Do not be afraid ... " That's a refrain that echoes throughout Scripture. The Lord gives the same message to Moses, Joshua, Isaiah, and Jeremiah: "Do not be afraid." Like all those giants

of the faith, Paul had good reason to be afraid; the opposition was strong. But the Lord tells him he need not be.

Paul was in a position to hear these words from Jesus[4] because he was depending on the Holy Spirit. It was this place of entire dependence that made it possible for him to hear from Jesus. Are you in a place of dependence? Are you in a position that enables you to hear the words of Jesus?

Jesus goes on to say to Paul, *"do not be silent."* Is it possible that Paul could have felt tempted to stop preaching the Gospel? Jesus gives Paul assurance that he should *"keep on speaking"* because he will be safe in Corinth. Being silent now would be disobedience to his calling.

We **stay the course** because we are connected to Jesus and connected to fellow believers. We are connected to Jesus and to our fellow soldiers with an intention: we believe He has a plan for the world and we want to be part of it. We are "in Christ" for the salvation of the world. These words from Jesus indicate the importance of this mission. *"For I am with you, and no one is going to attack and harm you, because I have many people in this city."* Not only does Jesus say *"For I am with you,"* but he says Paul will be free from harm because *"I have many people in this city."* (18:10) The team has grown exponentially! The Lord now has many people in this "sin city."

Immediately after Paul's encounter with Jesus, Luke shows that Paul **stayed the course;** he followed God's agenda, not his own. *"So Paul stayed in Corinth for a year and a half, teaching them the word of God."* (18:11) What happened as the Gospel spread throughout Corinth was powerful. But the new church

---

4   Every commentator that I read says that *"the Lord"* in this passage must be Jesus because it reads like Paul's other encounters with Jesus. It is significant that this setting parallels Old Testament theophanies.

wasn't perfect, as we learn from Paul's two letters to the believers there. Paul continued to **stay the course** with the church he had helped to birth in the city. Without those letters, we would have a large hole in our understanding of Paul's commitment and the implications of the Gospel's working out in the real world.

Paul stayed the course in Corinth because he was connected to a synergistic community; he was connected to the exalted Jesus; and he was connected to the mission that Jesus has for the world. We have the opportunity to be connected in this same way. Will we **stay the course** for the sake of the mission—connected with one another and with Jesus?

Chapter 20

Living Out the Course

Acts 20:13–38

F inish well. I've heard these two powerful words used on many occasions. But there was one time when I heard them in a fresh way. A couple of weeks before we were commissioned as Salvation Army officers, Commissioner Jim Osborne, former national commander, gave a series of lectures at the training school on ministry as an officer. The lecture titled "Finish Well" seemed an odd one to include in the series. At that point Abby and I were 40 years from finishing or retiring; we hadn't even begun yet! But I can still recall Osborne's passionate plea not to coast our way to retirement, but to **stay the course** and finish well.

Throughout this section, we have seen how Paul **stayed the course** despite frustration, provocation, and persecution. Now he has another challenge: he must bid farewell to a church he has spent three years building up.

Like the church at Corinth, the church at Ephesus was of

137

enormous significance in Paul's ministry. Let's recap the story of his time there, as told in Acts 19. When he first arrived, he found a group of disciples already there and laid hands on them so they received the fullness of the Holy Spirit. (19:1–7) Then he spoke boldly for three months in the synagogue. But some people *"became obstinate; they refused to believe and publicly maligned the Way."* So Paul instead concentrated on working with the disciples and having daily discussions in a lecture hall, *"so that all the Jews and Greeks who lived in the province of Asia heard the word of the Lord."* (19:8–10) God did such extraordinary miracles through Paul that *"even handkerchiefs and aprons that had touched him"* cured sick people. (19:11–12) Some people who were attempting to cast out demons *"in the name of the Jesus whom Paul preaches"* were defeated. (19:13–16) Then some agitators started riots. They were in the business of making idols of the goddess Artemis, and they were losing money because so many people were following the Way. Paul and two brothers in the faith were soon in great danger from the mob, but finally a city official quieted things down, and Paul was able to leave. (19:23–20:1)

Paul spent the next two years in Macedonia and Greece, encouraging the believers in Philippi, Berea, Thessalonica, and Corinth. Now he is on board ship, on the first leg of a journey to Jerusalem, sailing down the eastern shore of the Aegean Sea. The city of Ephesus is on that eastern shore.

Paul had **lived out the course** in Ephesus in the face of opposition from people in the synagogue, demonic forces, and idol worshipers. And because of his faithfulness and persistence in preaching and teaching, large numbers of people came to belief in the Lord Jesus. So nothing would please him more than to visit the church he had birthed. But instead, *"Paul decided to sail past Ephesus ... for he was in a hurry to reach Jerusalem, if possible, by the day of Pentecost."* Still, he can't go on without at least spending some time with the elders of the Ephesian church. So he sends a message to them to meet him at his ship. (20:16–17)

Paul Pours Out His Soul

So far in Acts, we have read accounts of Paul speaking in synagogues, to the intellectual elite in Athens, and before political leaders. The speech Luke records in Acts 20 is the only one given to an audience of believers. To the savvy Bible reader, the speech feels very familiar, because it sounds like Paul's letters, which were written to believers. We know Paul is very close with this group of leaders because he begins the speech by saying, *"You know how I lived the whole time I was with you ... "* He then pours out his soul as he talks about how he *"served the Lord with great humility and with tears and in the midst of severe testing ... "* (20:18–19)

This is a sad scene, one charged with emotion. The Ephesian elders had been welcomed into the Kingdom of God under Paul's evangelistic leadership, and he had taken great care to teach them what it meant to be followers of Jesus, to **live out the course** themselves. He had *"not hesitated to preach anything that would be helpful to you but have taught you publicly and from house to house. I have declared to both Jews and Greeks that they must turn to God in repentance and have faith in our Lord Jesus."* (20:20–21)

This verse is the basis for the Salvation Army's article of faith that says, "We believe that repentance toward God, faith in Lord Jesus Christ and regeneration by the Holy Spirit are necessary to salvation." John Wesley says, in a note on verse 21, "The very first motion of the soul toward God is a kind of repentance."[1] This means that we move away from ourselves, our own selfish egos, to a Kingdom focus.

Paul echoes that idea when he explains how he's ready for the trials—including hardship and prison—that he believes lie ahead of him in Jerusalem. *" ... I consider my life worth nothing to me; my only aim is to finish the race and complete the task the Lord Jesus has given me—the task of testifying to the good news of God's grace."* (20:22–24) Paul's *"only aim"* is to *"finish the race,"* to run it faithfully. E. Stanley Jones says that unless we dedicate our lives to the course God has laid out for us, we will suffer an "incurable malady," which is "unsurrendered egocentricity." Jones is saying that if we are not running the race, **living out the course** with Him, we will be "egocentrically focused." In other words, all we will care about is ourselves.

Losing a Teacher

Then the elders hear Paul say, *"Now I know that none of you among whom I have gone about preaching the kingdom will ever see me again."* (20:25) Imagine how intensely they must be listening now. Imagine the thoughts swirling through their minds as they store up memories they will carry for the rest of their lives: "What was his message in that last sermon I heard him preach?" "What should I ask him?" "What will we do without him?"

You can probably name several people—a mentor, a teacher, a pastor, a friend—who took the time to speak into your life and help you develop a deeper spiritual life. When you come to a time when you realize that one of these people of giant significance to you will no longer be available—because of illness, physical absence, or death—you deeply feel the loss.

---

1   John Wesley, *Explanatory Notes on the New Testament* (London: The Epworth Press. 1954).

As we walk through this passage in which Paul encourages and exhorts the Ephesian elders, we can relate to their sadness, but with them, we hear a ring of hope in his words.

Paul says to the elders that he is *"innocent of the blood of any of you"* because *"I have not hesitated to proclaim to you the whole will of God."* Paul has been obedient to his call; he has **lived out the course** for them. Then he challenges them, *"Keep watch over yourselves and all the flock of which the Holy Spirit has made you overseers. Be shepherds of the church of God, which he bought with his own blood."* He is calling those he has taught to take his place in leading the church. They will need to be strong, he warns, because *"savage wolves will come in among you and will not spare the flock."* Some of these "wolves" will be outsiders with evil intent, seeking to destroy the church. But, he tells them, *"Even from your own number men will arise and distort the truth in order to draw away disciples after them[selves.]"* Notice how Paul says that they will draw *"disciples after them[selves]."* These men will have their own agendas, their own plans; they will not be following God's plan. Consequently, the Ephesians must take care to **live out the course** that is been laid out for them by God—even when opposition comes. (20:26–30)

As a benediction, Paul says, *"Now I commit you to God and to the word of his grace, which can build you up and give you an inheritance among all those who are sanctified."* (20:32) Even though the elders are facing Paul's departure, they have the Word of God's grace to sustain them. It is in the community of sanctified believers that they will find their support and nurture others who have experienced God's grace.

The Ephesian elders will not see their shepherd again, but they have an inheritance. They have God's grace, a course to live out with the Spirit to guide them, a community of sanctified believers, and a mission that is far more important than their lives. They have a race to run.

At the end of this scene, we have a beautiful picture of the response of the elders. *"When Paul had finished speaking, he knelt down with all of them and prayed. They all wept as they embraced him and kissed him. What grieved them most was the statement that they would never see his face again. Then they accompanied him to the ship."* (20:36–38)

The Ephesian Christians had to deal with deep grief because they would never see their beloved teacher again. I can imagine that their weeping continued as Paul's ship sailed out of sight. But they knew that what their teacher had said was true: They still had God's grace with them. When our spiritual heroes are absent, we too will grieve, but we must remember that the God they pointed us to is not absent. His work and His grace in our lives continue.

Never Alone

The Ephesians are not alone. They have the Lord and one another. So do we. We are also promised a *"great cloud of witnesses"* to cheer us on. (Hebrews 12:1) Just as the memory of Paul's teaching will be fresh in the minds of the believers in the Ephesian church, the memories of those who have gone before us still speak into our lives.

Every now and then the Spirit uses my memories of both my grandfathers and of my forebears in the faith to encourage me. As I face the challenges that I experience what Jim Knaggs and Stephen Court call the "vocational extremism" of Salvation Army officership, the Holy Spirit helps me remember Grandpa Miller saying, in his New York accent, "Go get 'em, Ange," and

I am encouraged to **live out the course** laid before me. Or I hear my wife's grandfather, Dr. Billy Key, a man of holy influence, saying, "Run the race. Preach the word in season and out of season," and I am encouraged to **live out the course.** I read about the last words of John Wesley on his deathbed, "Best of all, God is with us," and I am encouraged to **live out the course.** I hear William Booth charging us to "fight to the very end," and I am encouraged to **live out the course.** These "witnesses" give me courage in the fight, and the words of Paul and my heroes challenge me to **live out the course.** It is when I commit myself to living my life focused on what God has for me that I begin to see its focus and purpose. I don't "practice" the course, or "play" the course. I put my life into **living out the course** so that in the end, I will "finish well." I pray it will be said of me, "He **stayed the course**." Will you be one who will "live out the course" and "finish well"?

Chapter 21

Paul on Trial

Acts 21– 26

Generally, in this book, we have moved slowly through one chapter of Acts at a time. The opposite will happen here; we will move quickly through six chapters. Through such a survey, we can see the big picture of Paul's experiences during an extended time of opposition and trial. At every turn, he could have abandoned the path God had laid out for him, but he **stayed the course**.

In the previous chapter of this book, we discussed Paul's resolute commitment to getting to Jerusalem even though he knew that he faced imprisonment when he got there. He said with determination to the Ephesian elders, *"Now, compelled by the Spirit, I am going to Jerusalem, not knowing what will happen to me there. I only know that in every city the Holy Spirit warns me that prison and hardships are facing me."* (20:22–23) Soon after Paul arrived in Jerusalem, his stand for bringing the Gospel to the Gentiles put him at the center of a riot that led to his arrest. (21:27–36) Over the next two and a half years, he was imprisoned in Jerusalem, then Caesarea. During this time (Acts 21–26), he defended himself before an angry mob and underwent four trials. From the point of his arrest and on through the book of Acts, Paul was a prisoner.

Paul first made his defense before a Jewish crowd who would have killed him but for some Roman soldiers who rescued him from the angry mob by arresting him. Before the soldiers took Paul into the barracks, he asked permission to speak to the crowd. After that encounter (more on that later), the soldiers ordered Paul into the barracks and were about to flog and interrogate him, when he invoked his Roman citizenship. (21:37–22:29)

That saved Paul from a beating; but the Roman commander still wanted to find out why the Jews were so opposed to him, so he ordered that Paul appear before the Sanhedrin (the rulers of the Jews in Jerusalem): trial number one. (22:30–23:10) Then, after a plot by some Jews to kill him failed, he was taken by night, under the protection of more than 400 guards, to the Roman provincial capital of Caesarea. There, as a Roman citizen, Paul was brought before Felix, the Roman governor, where he faced charges brought by Ananias, the Jewish high priest: trial number two. (23:12–24; 24:1–22)

Paul's case remained undecided, so he languished in prison for two years until a new governor, Festus, arrived. The chief priests and Jewish leaders pushed to have Paul transferred to Jerusalem; their plan was to kill him in an ambush. But Festus told the Jewish leaders that if they wanted to state their case against Paul, they would have to come to Caesarea. There, in trial number three, Festus asked Paul if he would be willing to go to Jerusalem to face his accusers there. But Paul refused, invoking his right as a Roman citizen and appealing to Caesar. *"To Caesar you will go!"* said Festus. (25:1–12)

In the meantime, King Agrippa II, a great–grandson of Herod the Great appointed by Rome to oversee the Jews, came to pay his respects to Festus, who discussed Paul's case with him. Paul then underwent trial number four before Agrippa, his wife, Bernice, and Festus (25:13–26:32).

At any point through all of these trials, Paul could have given in to the temptation to escape from persecution. As we look at some of the ways he might have done that but **stayed the course** instead, we can find encouragement to remain faithful through our own trials.

Paul could have taken the easy way out and kept his mouth shut. Maybe the thought went through his mind that if he stayed quiet, he could be set free and continue his missionary endeavors. He could have used an "end–justifies–the–means" argument. The end, his freedom, could give him the opportunity to continue his powerful ministry. But the means to that end would be putting a lid on his convictions about his mission to the Gentiles. Standing before the mob in Jerusalem, Paul chose to speak in Aramaic, their everyday language, and *"they became very quiet."* (22:2) He went on to give them his credentials as a follower of the great Rabbi Gamaliel, trained in the Law, zealous for God, and working with the high priest. The crowd was with him. But Paul couldn't help himself. He had to report what the Lord had told him: *"Go; I will send you far away to the Gentiles."* That did it for the mob. They had had it with Paul. They shouted, *"Rid the earth of him! He's not fit to live!"* (22:21–22)

Even in the face of his own possible death, Paul couldn't keep his mouth shut. He had to speak the truth. Luke records a similar incident in the life of Jesus. When He went "home" to Nazareth, the people were impressed by his words in the synagogue. But when he said that prophets were seldom accepted by their own people and reminded them that in the days of Elijah and Elisha, God's blessings had been extended to the Gentiles, the people of his once–affirming hometown tried to throw him over a cliff. (Luke 4:14–30)

In his trial before the Sanhedrin, Paul faced physical and emotional trauma. Yet, as Luke reports, *"Paul looked straight at the Sanhedrin and said, 'My brothers, I have fulfilled my duty to God in all good conscience to this day.'"* Again, in that moment, Paul could have kept quiet. Instead, Paul voiced his convictions and the high priest had him punched in the mouth for it. (23:1–2)

An Oregon man named Jason Johnson had struggled most of his life with addiction to drugs. At The Salvation Army's Adult Rehabilitation Center (ARC) in Portland, he found victory over his addiction and gave his life to Christ. He completed an intensive six–month work therapy program and received a GED as well.

Jason's next goal was to pursue a college education, beginning at Umpqua Community College in Roseburg. Just a few days into this chapter of his life, on October 1, 2015, another student, Chris Harper–Mercer, attacked the college. According to a news report on KTLA-TV, Harper–Mercer asked people to stand and say whether they were Christians, then executed them. Though we don't know if Jason was one of those who stood, we do know he was killed that day and that afterward, his family said he was "proud to be a Christian." So it's likely that Jason was martyred because he identified himself with Jesus. He **stayed the course** even when it meant he would lose his life.

We might not face such dramatic encounters as Paul and Jason Johnson did. But in everyday situations, are we tempted to take the easy way out and keep our mouths shut? We need to be ready to "name the Name" of Jesus, no matter what the cost.

Paul could have left well enough alone. As he stood before the Sanhedrin, Paul said, *"My brothers, I am a Pharisee, descended from Pharisees."* He could have stood on that reputation and said nothing more. But he went on, *"I stand on trial because of the hope of the resurrection of the dead."* (23:6) Paul knew full well what he was doing. The Pharisees, who believed that the dead would be resurrected, were instantly on his side. But the Sadducees, who believed that there was no resurrection—nor any angels or spirits—were so incensed by Paul's statement that a violent dispute broke out. The Roman commander was afraid that Paul would be *"torn to pieces."* (23:10) The reality of the Resurrection of Jesus was something that Paul couldn't deny. He couldn't leave well enough alone and stand on his credentials; he had to commit himself to the full truth that was guiding his course.

It was Paul's faithfulness in the midst of this persecution that put him in a position to hear from God. The Lord *"stood near Paul"* in the barracks saying, *"'Take courage! As you have testified about me in Jerusalem, so you must also testify in Rome.'"* (23:11)

In his trial before Festus, Paul could have left well enough alone by not appealing to Caesar. As King Agrippa said to Festus, *"This man could have been set free if he had not appealed to Caesar."* (26:32) But Paul knew his marching orders were to go to Rome and testify there.

Staying the course means being willing to stick our necks out, to take the hard road, to follow the path the Lord has marked out for us. When William and Catherine Booth left the ministry of the Methodist New Connection in 1861, they didn't immediately enter successful ministry in the East End of London. The Booth family had several challenging years as they followed God's path; they later called them "the wilderness years."

With four kids in tow, the Booths moved into Catherine's parents' house in London. They believed God had called them to preach to "the masses," and that could not happen within the New Connection system. Its leaders thought highly of Booth, and they wanted to give him a better appointment that would enable him to "climb the ladder" of their denomination. Certainly, if the Booths had left well enough alone, they would have been more comfortable in life and even successful in ministry within that church. They wouldn't have had to struggle to make ends meet, nor move in with Catherine's parents. But the Booths, convinced of what God's path was for their lives, endured hardship as they **stayed the course.** It's likely that you wouldn't be reading these pages if William and Catherine had left well enough alone.

Finally, **Paul could have questioned himself and been tempted to think he was wrong.** During the years of his trials, Paul experienced significant opposition from all layers of society. His contemporaries and friends in the Jewish community opposed him, as did the Jewish ruling body, the Sanhedrin. Centurions, military commanders, Roman bureaucrats, and even a king opposed him. He was slapped, punched, beaten, threatened, imprisoned, humiliated, and pushed around by the power holders of his day. Could he have thought while sitting in a jail cell, "My life is such a mess. Maybe that means I'm not doing the right thing, and I should just give up"?

In a previous appointment where we served, there was a couple, former addicts, who became engaged in the life and activity of the corps. This couple came to Christ and went through the first level of a discipleship course. They were enrolled as soldiers by a Salvation Army leader during an energetic ceremony and became local leaders. During this "honeymoon" phase of their Christian lives, they had temporary relief from some of the challenges in their lives. Then opposition came. Their addictions strongly tempted them; one of them faced a difficult medical condition; and something went wrong with his job. More temptations came and, I'm sad to report, they succumbed. Their trust in God flagged, and they slipped away from a "continued obedient faith" in Christ. When opposition hit their life, they backpedaled and gave up on their commitment to Jesus.

I believe that when Jesus enters our lives, the Holy Spirit empowers us to be "better at life"; we have the chance to experience what "true life" is. But that doesn't mean we won't face opposition. If we are following God's course for our lives, we should expect it. It's what we do next that counts.

Despite opposition from every side, Paul didn't give up because he knew he was connected to the hope of the world—the resurrected Jesus. Throughout Paul's speeches, it is that hope that Paul keeps invoking. He said to the Sanhedrin, *"I stand on trial because of the hope of the resurrection of the dead."* (23:6) Speaking before Felix, he said,

> *'I admit that I worship the God of our ancestors as a follower of the Way, which they call a sect. I believe everything that is in accordance with the Law and that is written in the Prophets, and I have the same hope in God as these men themselves have, that there will be a resurrection of both the righteous and the wicked.'* (24:14–15)

Then, speaking to Festus and Agrippa, he said, "'And now it is <u>because of my hope</u> and what God has promised our ancestors that I am on trial today. … King Agrippa, it is <u>because of this hope</u> that the Jews are accusing me.'" (26:6–7)

It was this hope that called Paul to risk challenging King Agrippa.

> 'King Agrippa, do you believe the prophets? I know you do.'
>
> Then Agrippa said to Paul, 'Do you think that in such a short time you can persuade me to be a Christian?'
>
> Paul replied, 'Short time or long—I pray to God that not only you but all who are listening to me today may become what I am, except for these chains.' (26:27–29)

Paul's hope for the world wouldn't allow him to give up when opposition came at him full force. What about us? When things are going wrong, when opposition comes, will we stand up and testify to the hope of the world? Will we have courage to witness to others, even those who have power over us?

If we want to **stay the course,** we must not take the easy way out and keep our mouths shut. We must not be content to leave well enough alone. And we must not be tempted to think that we are wrong about our convictions. With the help of the Holy Spirit, we must, like Paul, have the courage to testify to what we believe.

Chapter 22

Safe Through the Storm

Acts 27–28:10

I am impressed by soccer players and long–distance runners. Two of the most popular American sports, football and base-ball, require only short bursts of running. But soccer and dis-tance running involve running for hours. These sports require a resolute focus; competitors have to **stay the course.**

At the end of Acts, Paul has been running a long time, with great endurance. He could have stopped at any time; after all, he did enjoy victories in Antioch, Philippi, Berea, Corinth, and Ephesus. Instead he keeps going, with the Lord's leading. As a Salvation Army today, we could easily look back on the victories of 150 years of ministry and be satisfied. But I believe we are called to keep running the race, to **stay the course**—both as an Army and as individual believers—even when severe trials come.

When we left off in the previous chapter, Paul had faced *literal* trials before the Jewish Sanhedrin, Roman leaders Felix and Festus, and the Jewish King Agrippa. Paul, whose only "crime" was teaching about Jesus as Messiah, could have been set free. But because God had told him he would testify about the Lord in Rome, he made an appeal to be tried before Caesar (25:11).

In the part of Acts we come to now, we read about Paul's journey to Italy by ship. Things went well for some time; at one stop, in Sidon, the prisoner Paul was allowed to *"go to his friends so they might provide for his needs."* (27:3) The first ship sailed across the open sea for a time without trouble. Then the prisoners and the soldiers guarding them boarded another ship bound for Italy. The wind was against them, so they were forced to alter course and anchor off the island of Crete. The sailors were anxious to move on, but Paul warned them, *"Men, I can see that our voyage is going to be disastrous and bring great loss to ship and cargo, and to our own lives also."* (27:10) Paul was no sailor, but at this point, he was a prophet. He warned the sailors, "Trouble is coming!"

Expect the Storm to Come[1]

Trouble is always right there with us. Jesus forewarned the disciples in John 16:33, *"In this world, you will have trouble."* The Lord didn't beat around the bush! But He followed that tough warning with a sharply contrasting promise: *"Take heart! I have overcome the world."* Jesus spoke these powerful words just before He was betrayed, before Peter denied Him, before He went to the Cross—and before He rose from the dead. At

---

1   The basic points made from here on were inspired by a sermon I heard from Carl Lentz, "I Was Born for This," given at LifeChurch.tv (available on YouTube).

this point in the Gospel narrative, Jesus was preparing to face a storm the likes of which none of us will ever experience. He had so much confidence in His own ultimate victory that He said we could count on Him to *"overcome the world"* for us. We serve an exalted Christ who sits at the right hand of the Father interceding on our behalf. We don't have to do it alone.

Like Jesus and Paul, we should expect storms to come and be ready for them. John Newton was a sailor in the British navy who eventually became a captain in the slave trade. Later in life, he repented of his sin and went into service for God. He wrote hundreds of hymns, including "Amazing Grace," perhaps the best–known Christian song of all time. I recently discovered a Newton hymn that I hadn't known before. This is a song that came from a man who knew the challenges of the sea:

> Begone, unbelief,
> My Saviour is near,
> And for my relief
> Will surely appear;
> By prayer let me wrestle,
> And he will perform;
> With Christ in the vessel,
> I smile at the storm.

"With Christ in the vessel, I smile at the storm." We can smile at the storms we face because Jesus is with us. I can almost hear Newton saying, "I smile at this storm because I know that it is an opportunity for me to experience God's deliverance." Are you prepared to embrace the challenges that come your way, knowing that God will use them to show you His grace and power?

We know that Jesus will be with us through the storm. But

sometimes we willfully sail into a storm that we could have avoided. In this story about Paul, the members of the ship's crew were deceived when a "gentle south wind" began to blow. They set sail, but it wasn't long before a hurricane–force wind, the "Northeaster," swept down from Crete. Luke writes: *"The ship was caught by the storm and could not head into the wind; so we gave way to it and were driven along."* (27:15) It was a perilous situation, and it was about to get worse. The sailors had to hoist the lifeboat on board, run ropes under the ship to hold it together, and lower the anchor to keep the ship steady in the face of the punishing winds.

"We took such a violent battering from the storm that the next day they began to throw the cargo overboard." (27:18) On the third day, the ship's tackle had to go. Then, *"When neither sun nor stars appeared for many days and the storm continued raging, we finally gave up all hope of being saved."* (27:20)

In the midst of the storm, Paul did something that seems rather rude—to say the least! *"After they had gone for a long time without food, Paul stood up before them and said: 'Men, you should have taken my advice not to sail from Crete; then you would have spared yourself this damage and loss.' "* (27:21) It's an "I–told–you–so" moment for Paul, delivered even as the men were starving. Why on earth would he do this? Because God had given him a prophetic word that could have saved the situation, and no one had listened. When Paul delivers his "I told you so," he's representing God, who often said to His people, "I told you so." Remember the disaster that followed when Israel demanded a king, against God's strong warning? In that situation, it was the prophet Samuel who delivered God's "I told you so." (The story is told in 1 Samuel 8 and 12.)

Have you ever received a clear word from God that you

shouldn't follow a certain path, yet you ignored it and went your own way? What happened? I'm guessing it was nothing good! If we willfully sail into the storm, we will surely find trouble. But thankfully, our Lord doesn't leave us there.

Expect to Get Through the Storm

Paul's next words to the soldiers and crew are much more encouraging.

> 'But now I urge you to keep up your courage, because not one of you will be lost; only the ship will be destroyed. Last night an angel of the God to whom I belong and whom I serve stood beside me and said "Do not be afraid, Paul." ' (27:22–24)

What an awesome testimony! Paul is saying, "My identity is found in God, and He has assured me that I need not fear." Maybe in the midst of your own storm, you simply need to hear those words, *"Do not be afraid."* Notice that the angel of the Lord calls Paul by name! I can hear that sentence with my name in it: "Do not be afraid, Andy." Can you hear it with your name in it? Jesus has overcome the world! So we can **expect to get through the storm**.

Remember, God had told Paul that he would testify in Rome, so God was going to be *sure* he got there. Now he is reminded of that and also receives a promise that everyone with him will be safe too. The angel said, *"You must stand trial before Caesar; and God has graciously given you the lives of all those who have sailed with you."* Paul reassures everyone, *"So keep your courage, men, for I have faith in God that it will happen just as he told me."* But he adds, in another prophetic word, *"Nevertheless, we must run aground on some island."* (27:24-26) Paul didn't know which island; God hadn't given him that information. But he knew enough to say, in a very matter-of-fact way, "We'll be safe, but we'll be shipwrecked."

In our own lives, we sometimes receive an assurance from God—perhaps through the Bible or as we pray—that things will eventually be all right. We might feel a sense of peace, for example, that a loved one will be cured of cancer or be delivered from addiction. But we can also expect that in the meantime, there will be difficult days: The cancer treatments will take a toll; the addict may have to hit bottom before seeing a way up. "Shipwrecks" often happen before the storm is over.

With shipwreck imminent, Luke describes another seemingly odd thing that Paul did.

> Just before dawn Paul urged them all to eat. 'For the last fourteen days,' he said, 'you have been in constant suspense and have gone without food—you haven't eaten anything. Now I urge you to take some food. You need it to survive.' (27:33–34)

Eugene Peterson, in *The Message*, paraphrases that passage this way: *"Paul called everyone together and proposed breakfast."* Here's what I think Paul was getting at by "proposing breakfast." It's as if he was saying, "Let's be prepared to survive this storm. We're going to see this thing through." We too need to do things, such as feasting on the Word, that ready us to weather the storm. When we do, we show that we expect to get through the storm.

Carl Lentz, a pastor from New York City, said something that really struck me; at first, I didn't quite agree with it: "The storm you are facing may not be about you." It might be that God wants to master the storm through you, for the good of someone else.

You might not ever know, until eternity, how the storm you are experiencing was used for someone else's benefit. Maybe he's using your storm so that you can witness to somebody else in the midst of it.

Be ready. God wants to use you. If we recognize the fact that storms will come and prepare for them, knowing that God will protect us and guide us through them, we can also trust that God will use these experiences for our good or for the good of others.

Shake it Off

After the shipwreck, everyone on the ship was alive, just as Paul had promised. Now it seemed like it should be time for a break. And at first, it looked like that was happening. The people of Malta, where the survivors were stranded, showed them *"unusual kindness,"* building a fire to warm the cold, wet survivors. But then came more trouble.

> *Paul gathered a pile of brushwood and, as he put it on the fire, a viper, driven out by the heat, fastened itself on his hand. When the islanders saw the snake hanging from his hand, they said to each other, 'This man must be a murderer; for though he escaped from the sea, the goddess Justice has not allowed him to live.' But Paul shook the snake off into the fire and suffered no ill effects.* (28:3–5)

After all Paul has been through—beatings, prison, persecution, shipwreck—a snake bites him! Immediately **he shakes it off** and throws it into the fire. It isn't that he hasn't been bitten—he has. Trouble has assaulted him yet again. People are watching to see what will happen next. *"They expected him* *to swell up or suddenly fall dead."* They keep watching. When nothing happens, they think Paul must be a god. (28:6)

From the very beginning of the Bible, the snake represents evil incarnate. Sometimes, the evil one attacks us and even latches on. But we are people who, when we are attacked, can **shake it off.** How is that possible? The people of Malta assumed Paul was a god because the snakebite didn't make him sick or kill him. But Paul, who had trusted God to keep him safe through the storm, simply trusted Him again when the snake bit him. We too have the one true God, in Jesus, with us at all times by the power of the Holy Spirit. When He is with us, we can shake that snake (an attack from the enemy of our souls) off into the fire, where it will be consumed.

Yes, troubles, like the storm that shipwrecked Paul, will come in our lives. But we don't have to fear, for the Lord our God is with us. Yes, the evil one would like to stop us. But we don't have to fear, for the Lord our God is with us. And He has a plan for us, just as He had a plan for Paul. Despite everything that happened to him, Paul **stayed the course.** When we're in the midst of a storm, when circumstances seem to be more than we can bear, we need to trust God to get us through, for the sake of the fight. With God's help, we can **stay the course.**

Chapter 23

Hope Unchained

Acts 28:17–31

As Abby and I watched a Wilmore, Kentucky, sunset shift colors minute by minute, we realized that our time here was ticking to a close. Asbury University and Asbury Theological Seminary are in this small town. We had met here, dated here, lived in our first two apartments here, studied here, and spent our first few penny–pinching years of marriage here. That December we would graduate, and by the next Labor Day, we would be at The Salvation Army's training college. As we watched the sun set, we could have been sad that a formative time in our life was coming to an end. Yet we were not without hope, for we saw the potential of a family and ministry as officers on the horizon.

As we end this study in Acts, we need to reflect once more on our calling to **"take our place"** in spreading the Gospel; to **unite, move, and love** as the Church of Steel; and to **stay the course,** whatever difficult times may come. Our lives and the lives of the people we reach depend on it. Our journey through Acts has taught us much about who we must be for the Kingdom—and now we come to the conclusion.

Some people find the ending of Acts keenly unsatisfying. The book opened dramatically, with the ascension of Jesus and His admonition to His disciples to wait in Jerusalem for the Holy Spirit to come and give them power to *"be my witnesses in Jerusalem, and in all Judea and Samaria, and to the ends of the earth."* (1:8) Then came Pentecost, when the Spirit swept in with a mighty wind and tongues of fire and filled the "waiting host." We saw the newly filled Peter stand up to preach to those who crucified Jesus, and we saw an early church so unified that they fed on the Word and the apostles' teachings and became so united in love that they gave selflessly to one another, with the result that *"the Lord added to their number daily those who were being saved."* (2:42–47) We saw the work of the apostles, as they did what Jesus had done: spread the Word, healed the sick, and cast out demons. We watched as the church began to be persecuted and Stephen became its first martyr.

Starting with Acts 9, we have followed the story of Saul/ Paul. He is first a villain, a persecutor of Christians, then a hero (although a suspect one at first) who stands up to his own people and the Roman Empire. By turns, he is beaten, imprisoned, and left for dead. He undergoes several trials before the Sanhedrin, Roman governors, and even a king. He could have been set free, but because Jesus has told him he is to *"testify in Rome"* (23:11), he invokes his Roman citizenship and appeals to Caesar. (Acts 21–26; see Acts 20) On the way to Rome, he and his fellow prisoners and guards are shipwrecked on the island of Malta. Paul is bitten by a poisonous snake, and because he survives, is taken to be a god. While on the island, he has an opportunity to heal first one sick man, then everyone on the island who is sick. Then he is sent on his way on another ship bound for Rome. (27:27–28:11)

It's an exciting story, and we're looking forward to the climax. At first, it looks like we'll get a dramatic one. Christian brothers and sisters from Rome hear that Paul's ship has landed, and they come out from the city—some of them traveling more than 40 miles—to meet him. We learn that Paul *"thanked God and was encouraged"* by such a welcome. (28:15) But we don't hear anything of what Paul said to them. That's our first disappointment. After all, Paul has already written to the Roman Christians, and for us, that letter is one of the most important letters in human history because it outlines the depth of the Gospel message. In his letter, Paul has described his deep desire to see these fellow believers. So this first meeting, even if Paul is under prison guard, is something we would love to hear more about. But we don't. We only know that for the next two years, under "house arrest," Paul welcomed everyone who came to see him. (28:30)

What Luke does record about Paul's stay in Rome is his meeting with the local Jewish leaders, who haven't heard anything about his saga. He tells them, *"It is because of the hope of Israel that I am bound with this chain."* (28:20b) He fills them in about what has happened to him, and a familiar scenario repeats itself: Paul … *"witnessed to them from morning till evening, explaining about the kingdom of God, and from the Law of Moses and from the Prophets he tried to persuade them about Jesus. Some were convinced by what he said, but others would not believe."* (28:23b–24)

The Jewish leaders *"disagreed among themselves and began to leave"* after Paul's final statement quoting a prophecy of Isaiah, which he clearly meant should be applied to them: *"You will be ever hearing but never understanding; … ever seeing but never perceiving. For this people's heart has become calloused; they hardly hear with their ears and they have closed their eyes."* (28:25–27)

Because so many of his own people have not listened, Paul says to the Jewish leaders, *"Therefore I want you to know that God's salvation has been sent to the Gentiles, and they will listen!"* (28:28) Paul already knows this is true, and his success anticipates the spread of the Gospel *"to the ends of the earth."* (1:8)

The book of Acts ends on a hopeful note, as we hear that for two whole years, Paul *"proclaimed the kingdom of God and taught about the Lord Jesus Christ—with all boldness and without hindrance!"* (28:31)

But where is Paul's trial before Caesar? We know from other sources that Paul is killed, but Luke doesn't tell that story. Yet we have to believe that he concludes the book the way he does for a reason. Just as Paul *"proclaimed the kingdom of God and taught about the Lord Jesus Christ—with all boldness and without hindrance,"* so would Christians proclaim the Kingdom throughout the ages. Paul's time in Rome is not the end of the Christian story, but the beginning. As we leave him, Paul is *"bound with this chain … because of the hope of Israel."* It was this hope that called Paul to action, to "take his place" and "stay the course" in God's adventure.

As we seek to understand Paul's "hope"—and ours—it might be helpful to understand what that hope is not.

1. Our hope is not in political leaders.

As I write this chapter, the primary season is heating up for the 2016 presidential election. I am always amazed at how people in the congregations I have served have become invested in, and even passionate about, a presidential candidate.

Let's take a closer look at one campaign, the 2008 presidential race. Since we are several years removed from that heated election, we can probably look at it a little more coolly.

John McCain, the Republican candidate, ran on the slogan, "Country First." Yes, we're Americans and proud of it. But as Christians, our hope is not in our country; we have a different reality. Just as the Apostle Paul was not in chains for his country, our loyalties must lie much deeper.

Barack Obama's 2008 campaign emphasized "Hope and Change." If he was elected, the idea was, hope would thrive and things would change. Whatever you feel about Obama as a politician and President, you must recognize that our hope cannot be rooted in any political slogan or strategy. Our hope as Christians, as the song says, is "built on nothing less than Jesus' blood and righteousness."

2. Our hope is not in Christian leaders or Salvation Army officers.

Our hope cannot be grounded in our Christian leaders. In The Salvation Army, that means our hope cannot be in a corps officer, in divisional or territorial leaders, or in the General. Nor should our hope be placed in well-known Christian leaders or writers. Paul's hope, his reason for being shackled, was not a hope in Peter or James or Silas or Timothy. He kept an eye on one Leader: Jesus.

3. Our hope is not in our job or our paychecks.

Our hope will fail us if we look for it from our job or our pay-check. You might think, *If I could just sit in that seat, have that role, or occupy that office ... then I would be satisfied.* Is your hope, your reason for living, connected to making a certain amount of money or achieving a certain lifestyle? Your hope has to be in more than money or position or comfort; it has to be in something that outlasts such temporal things. Paul worked for a living as a tentmaker, but his work was a means to an end—serving the One who is the hope of the world.

4. Our hope is not in ourselves.

You can listen to all the motivational speakers in the world. You can center yourself, master yourself, focus yourself, train yourself, hope in yourself. But putting your hope in "self" alone will fail.

When our children were ages 5, 3, and 1, we took them to a park close to our house. Our boys were on their bikes. Titus, 3, had training wheels on his. Our 1–year–old daughter, Georgia, was in a stroller. I was pushing Georgia; Titus was riding next to me; and Abby and Andy IV were about 20 steps behind. We were climbing a hill and enjoying everything about the scene. The birds were singing, and it was as if you could hear Louis Armstrong singing, "What a wonderful world." It was perfect.

Then Titus crested the hill and quickly began gaining speed on the downslope. His training wheels bounced back and forth. Instead of pressing the brakes, his feet flew straight out to both sides. He was entirely out of control. I took off run-ning, still pushing Georgia, but the stroller's wheels started to bobble, and I struggled to catch up to Titus, who was headed for a small creek. As he screamed, I reached out desperately and stopped him. His bike fell over, and we were both on the ground. I was afraid he was hurt. Instead, while I was catching my breath, he jumped up and shouted, with his hands in the air, "That was AWESOME!" Then he ran back to Abby saying, "Whoa! Mommy, did you see that!?! I was going so fast down the hill ... then I saved myself."

Really, Titus, you "saved yourself"? With my heart still pounding, I looked at him and thought, *Well, I might not be my son's hero, but I did get a good illustration here.* (Preachers are always thinking like that; we just can't help it.) The incident taught me that when our world is headed out of control, it is a lie to think we can look to ourselves and find our salvation. Did Titus save himself? I don't think so. Neither can we find hope in ourselves.

As Paul finally has a chance to get the attention of the Jews in Rome, his fingers grasp the chain that binds him. He has experienced persecution, but he has also experienced the joy of justifying and sanctifying grace. I can imagine his eyes welling up with tears as he pleads with his fellow Israelites, *"It is because of the hope of Israel that I am bound with this chain."*

That hope was in the resurrected King Jesus, the Messiah who came to fulfill the hope of the Israelite people. The hope of Israel was, simply put, the redemption of the world. We don't place our hope in politicians, officers, possessions, money, acclaim, attention, public support, tradition, innovation, or ourselves. Our hope is "built on nothing less than Jesus' blood and righteousness." Our hope is in Jesus, the Messiah, the Redeemer, the Resurrection and the Life, and we are told that this is a hope that will not disappoint us. Hope doesn't float; it isn't a feeling; it is a reality based in the Resurrection of Jesus Christ.

Paul, while shackled by chains, calls people to action. He

has a hope to offer that breaks all chains! We must be like him, as he is in that last verse of Chapter 28: *"He proclaimed the kingdom of God and taught about the Lord Jesus Christ—with all boldness and without hindrance!"* Acts doesn't truly end, because it prompts us to keep "acting" on behalf of God's Kingdom. It's as if we become the 29th chapter of Acts.

It is because of hope that we act; it is for this hope that we live. The hope for the redemption of the world—Jesus—is connected to God's movement in our lives just as it was connected to God's movement in Paul's life. We also keep up the fight with urgency because the time approaches when Jesus will come again, as He promised he would.

One of the great theologians of our time, Jürgen Moltmann, writes that in the Christian hope, "the end is our beginning." What Moltmann is saying is that the great movement of God's salvation in the world culminates with the return of Christ, when God will make everything right and initiate His new creation.

The great ending of Acts and the hope of our world can be experienced even now if we will take our place in the Church of Steel, remain united in love, and stay the course. Because a time is coming—perhaps very soon—when Jesus will come again, this time as judge. In the meantime, let's move forward to the fight to bring the Gospel message *"to the ends of the earth."*

Ministry Resource
Two Dramatic Monologues

Being Agabus

A Dramatic Monologue

The setting: A jail cell in Jerusalem, 70 A.D. At stage left or right is a barred window.

Cast of characters: Agabus, a prophet. A Roman soldier.

Props: Large scroll; 'fanny–pack' belt; sheet of paper with writing on one side.

[Scene opens with spotlight on *Agabus*, holding scroll]

[Reads from the end of the scroll] *"For two whole years Paul stayed there in his own rented house and welcomed all who came to see him. He proclaimed the kingdom of God and taught about the Lord Jesus Christ—with all boldness and without hindrance!"*

[Rolls up scroll and "talks to it"] Ahh ... Luke, is that it? Come on, man ... you forgot to finish the story! This makes the end sound so great. But you forgot the part about Paul's going

171

before Caesar and being condemned to death. I guess you know what you're doing …

[Addresses audience] Oh, hi, pardon me. I'm just finishing a book written by my friend Luke that took me a while to read. Luke's kind of a "jack–of–all–trades" type of guy. He's not just your ordinary writer; he's a storyteller, a historian, and in his spare time, a doctor. He has been working on this **[Points to scroll]** for a long time. Lots of people have written about what happened during the years when Jesus was with us. Being the researcher and historian that he is, Luke wanted to give what he calls "an orderly account" of all the details about Jesus' birth, ministry, teachings, crucifixion, resurrection, and ascension. And Luke is the only one who also has written about how the church began and spread, starting at Pentecost.

Maybe you know all about that stuff. He sent me this note **[Pulls paper out of 'fanny–pack' belt and reads]:**

> *Dear Agabus,*
>
> *We had a great time together; you are a true friend in Christ. Thanks for helping me find the shepherds. You will see their story in the first volume. Sorry I couldn't include more of your story. I had to keep focused on Paul, but you will find yourself in here a few times.*
>
> *His Kingdom come, Luke*

[Turns to audience again] Agabus. That's me. You probably don't know who I am. Last time I spoke to a group they said, "Agabus, are you the guy who invented the abacus?" No, come on … I'm old, but not that old. That was invented by the

Chinese—who else, didn't they invent everything?—3,000 years before I was born.

Oh, back to Luke. We became great friends after we met in Jerusalem as the church was getting started there.

Jerusalem, that's my home town. I grew up there and went into the belt–making trade. ... Yes, I'm a belt maker. Don't laugh. Now look, almost all of you men in the room are wearing a belt, and a lot of the women too. Do you think these things come out of thin air? Just think of all the embarrassment that has been saved by my industry. People used to do things with just one hand; they needed the other to hold their pants up—or their togas together. **[Gestures to his own belt]** Without me, there would be a lot more embarrassing moments. My ad slogan is: "Belts by Agabus—You'd Cuss Without Us!"

Here's the story of how I came to know Jesus. My business partner and I were selling belts outside Jerusalem and I came upon a group of people. A crowd was gathered around this guy. He was healing people and talking about the "Kingdom of God." His message hit me right in my heart, and I found myself saying to Him, *"I will follow you wherever you go."* Jesus then said to me, *"Foxes have dens and birds have nests, but the Son of Man has no place to lay his head."* At the time, I was perplexed by what He meant, but later, I realized that He was saying He was so focused on his task that He couldn't have a home; it didn't matter where He slept. I thought He meant that I should be like Him. So I gave up my belt–making shop in Jerusalem and followed Him.

I was like "Where's Waldo?" in many other scenes Luke describes in his book. I was one of the 72 Jesus sent out to preach. I was one of the 500 Jesus appeared to after His resurrection. I was there on the day of Pentecost when the Holy Spirit came. Whoa! What a day *that* was! I would love to tell you about everything I experienced, but I want to mention one dramatic event in my own life that Luke decided to put in his book.

You should know that I'm a pretty funny guy. Luke knows that; he's heard all my jokes. But I sure don't come across that way in his book. It's like he's trying to paint me to be like Isaiah, Jeremiah, or some of the other prophets from the Scriptures.

But I do understand why he does that: God has given me the gift of prophecy. So many people get this gift confused, so let me tell you what it means. There are two ways I describe what I do. There is *forth*–telling and *fore*–telling. *Forth*–telling means I "tell it like it is." It's a spiritual gift, and most of the time when I use it, I am "setting people straight" in Jesus' name. Someone from your time who was a forth–telling prophet was the Rev. Dr. Martin Luther King, Jr. He spoke the truth and woke people up so that they marched for civil rights.

Fore–telling is when I predict something that will happen. Jesus did this … He foretold His death and resurrection (though I confess many of us didn't understand what He meant at the time).

Luke mentions me twice, and both times I did some foretelling. The first time, I was with a group that had come down from Jerusalem to Antioch, where we had heard Paul and Barnabas had been doing some awesome work. This is how Luke describes what happened. *"During this time some prophets came down from Jerusalem to Antioch. One of them, named Agabus, stood up and through the Spirit predicted that a severe famine would spread over the entire Roman world. (This happened during the reign of Claudius.)"* My prediction came true. This famine hit Jerusalem hard, and the church in Antioch took up a collection to help the Jerusalem church.

This was serious business, and Luke tells about in a very serious way. But does he ever mention my lighter side? Not at all. Does he even talk about the belts I made for everyone? Nope. Come on, Luke!

But still, we became good friends. I traveled with him part of the time he was doing his research. We were trying to find people who remembered Jesus' birth. As Luke mentioned in his note to me **[Shows note again]**, we went to Bethlehem and found some of the shepherds who came to worship the baby Jesus. One time after Luke interviewed them, he got really serious and said, "Agabus, has God ever given you a prophecy about me? A word to foretell about me?" I really hadn't heard anything from God about my friend, but I decided to play around with him. I put on a very serious face, reached my hand out to him, and said in a deep baritone voice, "Luke … Luke … I am your father."

Get it? He didn't either. I guess he hadn't heard about that other Luke—Skywalker, am I right? Sometimes I get weird glimpses into the future like that.

Back to reality. After a while, Luke went on the road with Paul, who was bringing people to God's Kingdom everywhere he went. I met up with them at Caesarea. They came to the house of Philip "the evangelist." Philip "had *four unmarried daughters who prophesied*" like me. When I came to the house, Luke and Paul had already been there for a while.

Luke told me about his journeys with Paul. Then he grabbed me and showed me his writing pad. I read his notes about Paul's speech to the Ephesian elders. It was so powerful! Then we got this idea: Maybe Paul should settle here in Caesarea. Just think, Philip the evangelist is here, and his daughters and I are prophetically gifted. Paul could set up a tent–making shop; I could make belts; and Luke could open a clinic. This could be the next seedbed for Paul, and we would get to be a part of it.

Not long after I got there, though, something different happened. Everyone had gathered in Philip's house, and as I walked in I stopped to take off my belt and laid it with the others near the door. As a belt–maker, I was looking at everyone else's belts. You see, in our time, belts were like your "fanny packs"; they carried all of our important documents and even money. Then the strangest thing happened. As I looked at one of them, the Spirit said, "I have a message about this belt." I questioned whether I had heard right. **[Looks upward]** "A message about a *belt?!* Really, Lord?" Then one of Philip's daughters gave me a hard stare, as if to say, "You'd better do what the Spirit is telling you." When I saw that, I knew I had to speak.

Luke got busy taking notes. All eyes were on me as I picked up the belt—it was a very long belt—and walked to the middle of the room. Then I did exactly what the Spirit had told me to do, not understanding why. I took the long belt and tied my feet and then my hands with it. Then I said, *"The Holy Spirit says, 'In this way the Jewish leaders in Jerusalem will bind the owner of this belt and will hand him over to the Gentiles.' "*

Luke put down his pen and said, "Whose belt is that?" The room was so silent you could hear a pin drop. Then Paul spoke up, with resolve in his voice, and said, "It's mine." Without a sound, I took the belt off and just held it there in front of me.

We couldn't believe it. What about all our plans? We knew that Paul was specially gifted for our time, and we wanted to protect him—and keep him right there in Caesarea. We all started talking at once, pleading with Paul to stay. When he started shaking his head, we said maybe he could go back to Corinth or Ephesus. Some of us were so upset we were crying.

But Paul broke in and shut us up. He grabbed the belt from me with righteous indignation, and said, *"Why are you weeping and breaking my heart? I am ready not only to be bound, but also to die in Jerusalem for the name of the Lord Jesus."*

We kept on arguing with him. "Think about the message and how much more useful you will be if you are alive!" we pleaded. He just wouldn't hear it, so finally *" … we gave up and said, 'The Lord's will be done.'"* We had often prayed, as Jesus taught us, *"Our Father in heaven, hallowed be your name, your kingdom come, your will be done … "* Now we had to live out that prayer. So Paul set out for Jerusalem. Luke went with him, and so did I.

We found a warm welcome there at first. Then, after about a week, sure enough, my prophecy began to come true. Paul was seized by the Jews, who said he was defying the Law and defiling the Temple. The Roman soldiers arrested him and bound him with chains, hand and foot. (Remember my belt?) That was the beginning of the end for Paul. Over the next few years, he would be imprisoned and tried before several leaders, and ultimately end up in Rome, where he would stand before Caesar. As my buddy Luke wrote at the end of Acts, Paul preached effectively there. Still, it was in Rome **[Hesitates, speaks with emotion]** that … that … that he was killed.

In the story Luke told about Jesus, it's interesting to read how He also persisted in going to Jerusalem even though He knew it was the beginning of the end for Him.

Jesus stayed the course. Paul stayed the course. They knew that they would die, but they stayed the course.

That got me thinking about myself. When I pray in Jesus' name, it doesn't mean that my life will be easier. Quite the opposite is often true. Since that time, I have felt led to take the same course that Paul and Jesus took. I have taken Paul's words to heart, *"I consider my life worth nothing to me; my only aim is to finish the race and complete the task the Lord Jesus has given me—the task of testifying to the good news of God's grace."*

[Moves to barred window] So I too am now in a prison in Jerusalem, where I have been bound. **[*Soldier* enters and wraps chains around *Agabus's* hands and feet]** I think this is the same cell where Paul was chained. Because of Jesus, I must stay the course. I have to, don't I? What about you? Will you stay the course with Him, no matter what comes?

[The following Scripture passages are quoted in this script: Acts 28:30–31; Luke 9:58; Acts 11:27–28; Acts 21:11; Acts 21:13; Acts 21:14; Matthew 6:9–10; Acts 20:24.]

Great Expectations for Titus

A Dramatic Monologue

The setting: A home on the island of Crete, mid–60s A.D.

Cast of characters: Titus, a pastor/teacher.

Props: Simple wooden chair, at center stage; standing mirror or wall mirror, set up near door at stage left; letter made up of two or three pages of thick, unlined paper, filled with writing.

[Titus enters stage left, drapes jacket over back of chair, and addresses audience] It has been nonstop for me today. I'm worn out. Paul was right when he said these Cretans are hard to deal with.

[Knocking is heard stage left; Titus goes to answer door, speaks to offstage visitors] Hello, can I help you? **[Pauses]** Yeah, I'm Titus. **[Pauses]** Yes, I traveled with Paul. You're who?

[Pauses] You're kidding! Zenas, you're the lawyer, right? And Apollos from Alexandria!

[Turns away from door to look in mirror, adjusts clothing and smooths hair, then turns back to doorway] Apollos, I'm your biggest fan! I heard about you from Priscilla and Aquila. Could you sign my copy of the Book of Hebrews? **[Pauses]** Come on, I know you must have written it. We all know it wasn't Paul! **[Pauses, a little disappointed, then listens]** Of course, you're tired. You'll have time for me in the morning?

[Reaches out stage left and takes letter] For me? Paul gave you this letter for me? You want me to see what it says? Sure ... OK. **[Reads aloud]** *"Paul, a servant of God and an apostle of Jesus Christ ... "* **[Looks up]** You want me to go further. *"To Titus, my true son in our common faith ... "* **[Looks up again]** Oh ... you want me to read the end of the letter. **[Turns to end of letter]** *"Do everything you can to help Zenas the lawyer and Apollos on their way and see that they have everything they need."* Oh ... I get it. **[Shouts out the door]** Hey, Linus! Take these guys' bags and get them set up in the guest house. OK, guys, see you in the morning. **[To audience]** Linus is the fellow who takes care of the place when I'm traveling, visiting the churches here on the island of Crete.

[Sits on chair] Finally, after six months I get word from Paul.

I've been working nonstop here these past six months. Crete is a big island; I have 160 miles of coastline to travel. It's beautiful here, but I've been working so hard, I really haven't had time to take in the sights. I came here with Paul—the guy you probably call the Apostle Paul. Me and my buddy Timothy call him P–daddy. I don't know if it's because Paul never had kids of his own, but he calls us his sons. Sometime he says "spiritual sons" or "sons in our common faith," but there have been plenty of times he has treated us like his real sons. When I first started preaching, Paul would get on me about the smallest things. He would say, "Titus, if you jump up and down all the time when you preach, people won't get the point you're trying to make."

I didn't mind being treated that way because my real dad died when I was 12. He was a great man, a businessman, the treasurer of our town—Iconium. The people there were always telling me I needed to grow up to take my dad's place as a leader. From the time I was a young boy, people would say, "We're expecting great things from you, Titus." So I studied hard and worked hard so I would be ready when the time came.

That all changed in just one day. Two Jewish men, Paul and Barnabas, came to town, and everyone was talking about what they were saying. I wanted to hear them for myself. But when I got to the center of town, the crowd was so big that I couldn't even see them. I finally found a spot on a staircase where I could see. Paul was pleading and arguing with the Jews of our town that their Messiah, Jesus, was killed for our sins—not just the sins of the Jews, but everyone's sins—the Greeks too.

This made some of the Jews angry, but there were other Jews who said Paul and Barnabas were making perfect sense. For me, the big moment came when Paul looked right at me ... at least it felt like he was looking right at me ... and he said, "Maybe you are trying hard to please everyone ... maybe you are trying to live up to the expectations of others. This Jesus has a plan for your life." Oh, wait, Paul talks about it right here in his letter to me.

[Reads] *The grace of God has appeared that offers salvation to all people. It teaches us to say 'No' to ungodliness and worldly passions, and to live self-controlled, upright and godly lives … Jesus Christ … gave himself for us to redeem us from all wickedness and to purify for himself a people that are his very own, eager to do what is good.*

So, you see, Jesus' coming to redeem us from sin and help us to do good was all grace, a gift from God. It meant I didn't have to try so hard to live up to the expectations of everyone else in town—or even my father. Jesus would help me to live up to God's expectations. I listened to Paul for hours, and I knew my life was never going to be the same. I felt the tears hit my fingers and fall on the steps below me. I went forward to the front of the crowd, and Barnabas came and prayed with me. I became a follower of Jesus. A few days later, Paul told us about the Holy Spirit, and after the Spirit filled me, my life was totally different. I sensed that God was going to use me for a higher purpose. The people of my town saw a difference in me. They had known me my whole life, and now I was a different Titus from the man they had come to expect.

Hundreds of us in Iconium began following Jesus, but there was a group who were furious with what Paul and Barnabas were teaching. One day we found out that some of these people were planning to stone them. We figured out a way for them to escape. Then, just as they were about to leave the city, Paul looked at me and said, "Titus, we need you." When he said this, it wasn't about the expectations of the people of my town. It wasn't even about Paul's expectations. It was about what God wanted and expected me to do. From that point on I traveled with Paul and Barnabas.

In those early days, there was still a lot of confusion about how Judaism was finding its fulfillment in the message of the Messiah Jesus. There were some who thought that to become a Christian, you had to become a Jew—if you weren't a Jew already. That seemed crazy to me because I became a follower of Jesus when I heard that this message was for me. My life was completely changed, and it was clear to everyone that God was using me.

So a meeting was called, a powwow of the big shots of the Church, to take place in Jerusalem. Paul and Barnabas were invited, and Paul asked me to come along. It was exciting to meet the great leaders Paul called the Pillars (although I'm not sure he called them that to their faces): Peter, John, and James. That's James, the brother of Jesus—who once had made fun of his great Brother and who was now one of the champions of the faith. Actually, there were two meetings in Jerusalem that week, both dealing with the same issue. Paul and Barnabas met privately with James, Peter, and John. Next there was a big council meeting where one group argued long and hard that non–Jews had to be circumcised and live according to the Law of Moses if they wanted to be Christians.

Then my moment came. Paul had me stand up. Everyone knew I was a Greek. If they didn't know it already, my name gave it away. Paul said, "Tell them your story, Titus." So I started to tell how God had saved me and used me in the work of the Gospel. While I was talking, it was as if everything went into slow motion. I was looking at this room full of Christians and realized I was the only one there who wasn't Jewish. I was the only one not circumcised. Everyone was looking at me.

Then a member of the group called the Judaizers said, "Titus, of course we believe your testimony. But think of how much more powerful your ministry would be if you were circumcised. There are Jews who won't even listen to you now because you haven't been. If you would submit to being circumcised, you would be fully a Christian." I was so confused. I could feel my heart pounding in my chest. After this the room broke into utter chaos. Then Paul spoke into my ear: "Titus, remember, you are my son in the faith." **[Reads]** *"When the kindness and love of God our Savior appeared, he saved us, not because of the righteous things we had done, but because of his mercy. He saved us through the washing of rebirth and renewal by the Holy Spirit ... having been justified by his grace ... "*

I knew then I could not live my life following the expectations of this group of Judaizers. I have been rescued from the expectations of others, and I live only for Christ. I stood up among the group and said: "The God who changed my life did so even though I wasn't circumcised, and I am not compelled by any outward sign but by the grace of God. I must give account to Him and be obedient to Him. I hear you, my dear Jewish brothers, but by not being circumcised I am an example to everyone that God's work in our lives is more important than this sign. My obedience to Him is a greater sign of faith than being bound by your expectations." As I sat down, the room was silent. Then James, the brother of Jesus, started clapping. Even some of the Judaizers started clapping. The final decision of the council was that it is not necessary to follow the Law of Moses to be a follower of Jesus.

The last few years have been an adventure. I have traveled far. Just a few months ago Paul and I arrived on this island. He has gone on westward toward Spain, but he asked me to stay here on Crete. I was beginning to feel like I could stay in this appointment forever. Now I get this letter. **[Reads]** *"As soon as I send Artemas or Tychicus to you, do your best to come to me at Nicopolis, because I have decided to winter there."*

I know how that's how it is with Paul, but sometimes it seems like I'm in some kind of Army. **[Pauses for reaction]** As soon as I get settled in one place, I get sent to another. But I will go, and not just to live up to the expectations of my leader, Paul. I know that I have to keep focused on the vision Jesus has for my life, on living up to His expectations. The only way I can do that is by being guided by His Word and His Spirit every day, all day long.

I don't know you guys, but are you struggling with the expectations of others? I could have lived my whole life trying to please the people of my home town. I could have given in to the Judaizers. But my allegiance is to Jesus and to being the Titus He has called me to be. He expects great things of me. And, with His help, I plan to live up to those expectations.

[The following passages from the book of Titus are quoted in this script: Titus 1:1,4; 3:13; 2:11–12, 13–14; 3:4–5, 7; 3:12.]

185

www.ingramcontent.com/pod-product-compliance
Lightning Source LLC
Chambersburg PA
CBHW070806050426
42452CB00011B/1910